100 Ideas for Primary Teachers:

Coding

Other titles in the 100 Ideas for Primary Teachers series:

100 Ideas for Primary Teachers:

Coding

Martin Burrett

BLOOMSBURY EDUCATION
LONDON   OXFORD   NEW YORK   NEW DELHI   SYDNEY

BLOOMSBURY EDUCATION
Bloomsbury Publishing Plc
50 Bedford Square, London, WC1B 3DP, UK

BLOOMSBURY, BLOOMSBURY EDUCATION and
the Diana logo are trademarks of Bloomsbury Publishing Plc

First published in Great Britain, 2018 by Bloomsbury Publishing Plc

A catalogue record for this book is available from the British Library

ISBN: PB: 978-1-4729-5137-3; ePDF: 978-1-4729-5139-7;
ePub: 978-1-4729-5138-0

2 4 6 8 10 9 7 5 3 1

Typeset by Newgen KnowledgeWorks Pvt. Ltd., Chennai, India
Printed and bound in the UK by CPI Group (UK) Ltd., Croydon CR0 4YY

All papers used by Bloomsbury Publishing Plc are natural, recyclable products
from wood grown in well-managed forests. The manufacturing processes
conform to the environmental regulations of the country of origin.

To find out more about our authors and books visit
www.bloomsbury.com and sign up for our newsletters.

Contents

Acknowledgements

Firstly, I would like to thank my family who have supported me during the writing of this book. Without their patience, it wouldn't have been possible.

I also would like to thank everyone who has supported my careers up until this point and have put up with my geeky obsession with educational technology.

I also have to thank the wonderful team at Bloomsbury for guiding me through the process and for their patience and expertise.

Introduction

Coding shapes the modern world. There is no part of life that it doesn't now touch, and we owe it to pupils to give them an advantage by teaching them the skills to code their own destiny, not for tomorrow, but to begin today.

Most of the ideas in this book can be realised using many different programming languages and coding platforms; *Microbit.org*, *Python.org* and JavaScript are all used and should be explored. However, I have based the vast majority of the instructional description, which is there to allow you to have the skills and coding prowess to instruct your class, using the Scratch platform from MIT, available at *scratch.mit. edu*. There were three reasons for this choice: it's widely used in schools already; it's free; and it allows users to share projects online, meaning that I can share examples with you, which you can then share with your class. Find the continually growing bank of my Scratch projects at *www.bloomsbury.com/100-ideas-primary-coding*. If you need additional help with any of the ideas in this book, or would like to suggest additional Scratch coding projects which I can add to my project bank, contact me on Twitter using *@ICTmagic*.

In writing, we become proficient by discovering what is right or wrong. We only become creative when we realise there isn't only *one right way*. The same is true of coding. I have offered many instructional descriptions about how you and your pupils could go about implementing the ideas within this book, but these are only some of the many different ways, and your pupils should be allowed to experiment, struggle, tinker, debug and achieve success using their own problem-solving skills to overcome difficulties rather than being shown 'the right way'.

With this in mind, enjoy your creative coding journey.

Martin Burrett, @ICTmagic

How to use this book

This book includes quick, easy and practical ideas and guidance for you to dip in and out of, to support you in planning and conducting effective coding classes.

Each idea includes:

- a catchy title, easy to refer to and share with your colleagues
- an interesting quote linked to the idea
- a summary of the idea in bold, making it easy to flick through the book and identify an idea you want to use at a glance
- a step-by-step guide to implementing the idea.

Each idea also includes one or more of the following:

Teaching tip

Practical tips and advice for how and how not to run the activity or put the idea into practice.

Taking it further

Ideas and advice for how to extend the idea or develop it further.

Bonus idea ★

There are 41 bonus ideas in this book that are extra exciting, extra original and extra interesting.

#hashtags
To prompt further exploration and discussion of the idea online.

Share how you use these ideas and find out what other practitioners have done using **#100ideas**.

Online resources for this book can be found at:
www.bloomsbury.com/100-ideas-primary-coding

Offline coding

Part 1

Decomposing robots

'My pupils find it hard to break tasks down into simple coding steps.'

Making algorithmic steps suitably simple for young learners is tricky, as there are many steps in everyday tasks that we do automatically. Decomposition takes a bit of robot thinking.

Naturally, all your pupils obey your every request without question every time. Put these well-honed skills to the test to help your pupils understand algorithms by breaking tasks down into very small steps, as coders do. In coding, this is known as *decomposition*.

Ask your pupils to form small groups of three or four. One pupil takes the role of a robot which follows the precise movement commands of the 'operators', the other group members, to complete a task which is unknown to the robot pupil. These can be everyday activities with a number of steps, but it's interesting to throw a few twists in for older pupils. Some examples include:

- making a sandwich, but with different fillings in precise places
- throwing a ball or beanbag into a bucket unseen, with operators guiding the power and direction of the throw.

Begin with fairly relaxed rules, but eventually ask the pupils to ensure their instructions are broken down into very small oral commands, as would be needed for a real robot command. This will need to be modelled. If the robot thinks the command is too complex, they can say 'ERROR' in their best robotic voice.

Build this into a game, similar to 'Simon says', where the operators must try to trick the robot into completing overly complex steps, without the robot saying 'ERROR', but with everyone still trying to complete the task.

#DecomposingRobot

X marks the spot

'I'm struggling to relate basic coding to real-world problems.'

Moving around the stage of a screen using code is simple, but pupils often use movement in a random way and fail to make this the focus to design something of value. Relate this idea to how we move in the real world.

Set sail on a treasure hunt. For best results, find an open space, such as a playground, sports field or hall (although this activity can be miniaturised and completed in the classroom if needed). Mark out a grid with chalk lines or cones.

In groups of two or three, give your pupils a map with an 'X' marking the spot where treasure is (allegedly) buried. To model the activity, you may wish to begin by plotting on the map itself, before venturing to the physical space. In the larger location, place a physical object that corresponds to the location of your treasure chest on the grid. The pupils must decide on which movements and turns to make across the grid to navigate from a starting point to the treasure before they begin, starting again and correcting or 'debugging' if needed. There is an opportunity to discuss standard units, which are just as important in computing as they are in maths.

Using a new map and treasure location, remove the physical object so that the pupils must rely solely on the map, and then repeat.

Next, each group must appoint an 'adventurer' to find the treasure without seeing the map. The adventurer will be guided only by the predetermined algorithmic commands of their teammates, which were worked out before they began to move. This can be extended by replacing verbal commands with written, pictorial or symbolic sequences.

Teaching tip

Make a grid with extra rows and columns to increase the difficulty of the task.

Taking it further

Increase the difficulty by including obstructions on the grid for the pupils to avoid or use commands to overcome, such as 'jump' and 'climb'.

Bonus idea ★

Add multiple waypoints to navigate to, and even clues about the next target to move towards at each point.

#XMarksSpot

Coded messages

'Why can't a computer speak my language, instead of me learning its language?'

Learning a coding language can be similar to learning a new foreign language, and translating one's thoughts and ideas into this new language takes some practice, especially as the computer cannot infer your meaning and cares little for your exaggerated hand gestures.

Taking it further

Digital devices use binary code in a few different ways, and you can explore these with your pupils. Binary is represented as a series of ones and zeros, which can signify the opening and closing of a switch, on or off, or data on a hard drive. They often appear in groups of eight to encode letters, numbers and other characters. The Internet uses fibre-optic cables to communicate by flashing lights rapidly on and off using binary, in a similar way to pupils using a torch to communicate across long distances.

Your pupils will be adept at communicating coded messages. Just ask your class to 'get in groups of ...' and watch the non-verbal negotiations begin. Visual communication skills are important for us in our everyday lives, but did you know that the Internet is built on technology which uses pulses or 'packets' of light to transmit over long distances and at the speed of light along fibre-optic cables?

Sit your pupils on two rows of chairs a few metres away from each other so that every pupil is facing a partner. Give one member of the pair a mini-whiteboard and pen. Play a drawing game, similar to Pictionary™, where you provide the drawer with a word or short message to communicate to their partner by drawing or writing alone. This should be simple.

Using a large space, such as a playground or hall, ask the pupils to repeat the activity again, but at a distance where small drawings cannot be seen. Ask them to convey another message across the distance. See what non-verbal solutions your pupils come up with. If they are struggling, guide the pupils to the solution of using one letter/number/emoji at a time to build a message over time. Relate this to how algorithmic instructions need to be encoded in a simple and predictable way so as to be understood by a computer and its software.

Tell the pupils that they will need to send a message over a few hundred metres. In small groups, ask them to devise a system to communicate over this distance before moving into their positions. Some possible ideas are:

- using a torch with a system like Morse or binary code
- encoding with flags
- tugs on a rope.

Give the sending group a message to send and ask that the receiving group decode the message. Give the groups a chance to refine their method. After a few attempts, add a competitive element by asking the groups to 'race' to encode and decode a message and deliver it back to the teacher. You could even try a relay message, where a number of groups must communicate a message from group to group with the first and final pupils being out of the line of sight.

Bonus idea

Investigate the internal communication systems within your school. Ask pupils to audit and assess how effective they are, and then research alternatives which may standardise them.

#CodedMessages

Fairground crane

'My pupils find it difficult to make clear step-by-step instructions.'

It can be very tricky for young children to take a step back, decompose and include all the information in instructions which humans can infer but computers cannot.

Use the correct syntax from a real coding language to create pre-planned instructions for a blindfolded operator to follow. Once the pupils are more familiar with coding, you could return to the fairground crane idea and create it digitally.

Begin by watching an online video of a fairground claw crane game with the volume turned down. As some pupils may not have seen one before, this is to show the class what they will be making. Explain that joviality has been scaled back due to budget cuts, so the pupils need to make and code their own claw crane game to provide some light relief.

Using a claw litter picker and a magnet on a string or rod (if you are really struggling, ask a pupil to lie on a table with their hand dangling over the edge), ask the pupils to practise picking up cuddly toys or soft objects.

Ask the pupils to do the same again, but this time wearing a woolly hat as a blindfold. They should find this much more difficult. Prompt pupils to think about how their classmates could help them. Their classmates can begin by doing this all verbally. Next, ask the pupils to use a non-verbal coding system to indicate direction and when to lower and pinch the claw, e.g. create 'buttons' by squeezing the shoulder or elbow of the claw operator.

Create a small grid on the floor and place the soft objects within some of the squares. Ask the group to create a sequence of operations for the crane operator to complete. Note these down on paper or using a whiteboard. Either continue with the 'squeezing buttons' or revert to verbal commands read from the notes.

#FairgroundCrane

Codify the class

'I'm looking for a quick and easy way to model and practise algorithms in my classroom.'

Building lists of instructions or algorithms that are decomposed enough and in the right order for a computer to understand is a little tricky, especially for young learners. The computer can't infer meaning or guess what they are attempting to do (despite that little animated paper clip's best efforts!)

Begin by asking your pupils to do various cleaning chores around the classroom. Hopefully, this will not be a new experience for them, so move on to asking them to do it while pretending to be robots. Call out a few simple, unbroken-down instructions which the pupils should complete without issue. Take a moment to marvel at how clean your classroom is looking for a change.

Discuss with your pupils how real robots need broken-down, decomposed instructions. Model this and allow them to try it. You can demonstrate using Apple's Siri or Amazon's Alexa. First, give them a few easy tasks, which they should complete easily, but then combine these tasks together and they will probably struggle.

Practise breaking down everyday tasks into minute detail. Pretend to be an easily misunderstanding, non-inferring robot and model some instructions given verbally by a pupil to complete an everyday task. Ensure that you do exactly as the pupil tells you, hopefully with comical results. Ask the pupils to refine their instructions until there is no ambiguity. Then ask the pupils to repeat the robot activity in small groups with a number of different everyday tasks.

> **Bonus idea** ★
>
> Make your tidying robots a regular feature of your classroom. Split the class up into four different types of robots for specialised tasks and assign them a colour. One colour identifies things to tidy and another colour directs the other two colours, who are assigned two different areas of the room.

#CodifyClass

Instruct me a picture

'How can I help my pupils become better at decomposition?'

Art has always been something which separates humans from machines. Indeed, much of the current discussion about artificial intelligence taking our jobs, both now and in the future, is about moving to careers in the creative sphere, which traditionally computers have found very hard to do.

Find or create some simple line drawings of everyday items. Children's colouring books are a good source of these. Make sure that the images cannot be seen through the paper from behind, and make sure the pupils cannot see the image being used in other groups. In pairs, ask the pupils to label themselves as a 'describer' or a 'scriber'. It will be the describer's job to explain to the scriber how to draw the picture without the scriber being able to see it. The scriber is not allowed to ask for clarification or for more details. Communication can only be one way. To start with, the describer will most likely give very generic explanations and descriptions, like 'draw a cat' or, if you are lucky, 'draw a cat standing up and looking alert'. After one attempt, the pictures should be compared. The pictures will inevitably be very different at this stage. Discuss with the pupils how they can refine and decompose their instructions for drawing the picture.

Just like when a coder is designing code for a computer, every step and every instruction needs to be logical and not using any inference, as computers cannot guess what you're trying to tell them. Instructions must be detailed. After this discussion, ask the pupils to attempt the task again with a different image. Hopefully, they will have honed their instructional skills, and the pictures will be more similar than before.

Bonus idea ★

Reverse this activity and explore machine intelligence with *quickdraw.withgoogle. com*, where the site will attempt to guess what you are drawing.

#InstructPicture

Coding exercise

'How can I integrate coding into my PE lessons?'

Many PE activities in schools rely on circuits and routines. Many teachers already incorporate signals into their PE lessons, such as a certain number of blows on the whistle to indicate to pupils to change what they are doing. But these instructions are usually given to them one at a time.

Create an apparatus circuit in the school hall consisting of mats, beams, cones, benches, etc. Ensure that the pupils are familiar with how to use the equipment safely if they have not used it before.

Ask the pupils to travel safely across the equipment in various ways. Pick out a few examples that you like and ask the children to showcase these to the rest of the class. Using a whiteboard or flip chart, ask the children to suggest pictorial ways of representing the action. Once you have decided on a symbol for each of the actions that children have showcased, put the symbols into a loop on the whiteboard. Tell the children that they can start at any point within the loop, but they must move clockwise around the activities as pictured on the board.

Once your class has completed the loop a few times, add an extra layer of complexity. Ask your pupils to encode new moves within each of the actions previously encoded within their group. These do not need to be consistent between the groups.

Finally, ask the pupils to create a routine and encode it themselves using their own symbols, which should be noted on paper. Swap notes and ask another group to interpret the actions.

Taking it further

Encode a dance routine in symbols and see if pupils can follow it. Take photos of each dance position and create a step-by-step guide as a flipbook or using PowerPoint slides.

Bonus idea ★

Give the class a completely new set of symbols which you have encoded before the lesson. These will signal the activities you want them to complete. Ask the pupils to interpret the symbols. Showcase and compare the different interpretations the groups come up with.

#CodingExercise

A-mazing games

'My class are struggling to understand algorithms and how to debug a list of instructions.'

New coders spend about as much time fixing code as they do creating it in the first place. Debugging requires many essential skills, and many of these are not technical. Logical thinking, consistency and patience are key. Things will go wrong and can always be improved. This is what software updates are all about.

Taking it further

Design a similar a-mazing game in a 3D digital environment like Minecraft. Use different-coloured blocks to denote particular actions.

In a game of snakes and ladders, it is difficult to see at the outset what die rolls a player needs to make to win. This only happens once the game is in play and, even then, players can see only a few moves into the future at most.

Use a draughts board or other grid and ask your pupils to create a maze or board game where the players must navigate around the board. Each of the squares should be coded with functions based on colours or symbols. For example, a blue square could mean turn left and move forward three spaces. The aim of the game is to get to a certain square. The designers must ensure that it is possible to reach the goal square. Once the game board has been designed, the groups swap over so that they are using another team's board.

Players of the game need to decide on a pre-planned route in a sequence before beginning. If the sequence is wrong, they must return to the start and *debug* their sequence. Because the coloured squares will take the players in directions which are difficult to see at the outset, the team will have no choice but to navigate by trial and improvement. The teams need to note down successful and unsuccessful steps to work towards their goal.

#AmazingGames

Lollipop letters

'I want to explore binary in an easy way.'

Binary code is how most devices communicate with one another. Coders will not write directly in binary code, yet it's useful to learn how impenetrable a computer's 'native language' is to humans and how our programming languages are halfway between how humans and how machines communicate.

Give pupils lollipop sticks or strips of paper. Tell them that they can put only one character on each stick. The aim of the activity is to convey a message to somebody else.

First, give them a fairly short message to relay. Your pupils will probably write one letter on each stick, which will make up the full message as a sentence.

Next, give your pupils a different message to relay to another group, but this time tell them that they are only allowed to use consonants. They will probably do exactly as they did before, but miss out the vowels. Up to this point, the children have been using their own language, albeit slightly adapted based on the conditions you have imposed.

Next, give your pupils yet another short message to communicate. This time the pupils can only use a single digital number on each stick, but they can also create a codebook to ensure that the receiving group understands the code the message is written in. If your pupils need a prompt, they may consider assigning each letter of the alphabet a two-digit number which is communicated using two sticks grouped in pairs.

For the final message, your pupils are only allowed to use either a red lollipop stick or a blue one – like the ones and zeros of binary. Your pupils must devise a way to code and create a codebook to convey the message to another group.

Teaching tip

Ensure that your pupils stumble across the idea, similar to Morse code, of using three or four sticks grouped together to encode one character.

Bonus idea ★

Messages don't have to be visual. Ask your pupils to encode words as sounds. Begin with letter associations, such as a dog barking for the letter D, and ask your pupils to make the sounds to convey short words one letter at a time. Progress to musical sounds to denote the consonants, and finally try binary with just two musical notes.

#LolliLetters

Rubbish robots

'How can I make a set of cheap robots so my pupils can practise a sequence of commands?'

Electronics are getting cheaper all the time, but they are still hugely expensive, especially when you need to buy 30 or more for a class set. So, the trick here is not to use electronics at all.

Dip into your hoarded collection of it-might-be-useful-one-day items, which all teachers have and seem reluctant to part with. Ask your pupils to collect clean, recycled rubbish which might be useful in building a rubbish robot.

When building the robots, ensure that they have a sturdy base so they don't fall over. They should be squat and have a flat bottom, so a milk container filled with something to weigh it down might make a suitable item to build on. You will need to ensure that the robots have all the capabilities to complete the task you set for them later, e.g. moving arms or a scoop. A little decoration to make the robot look more like a classic robot is a nice touch. Use glued-on paper, bottle caps or paint to give it the right look.

Once complete, the robots (and children) must receive training in how to be good robots before leaving the 'factory'. Take the robots through a few verbal commands, signalling the children to move their otherwise inanimate robots. Move on to sequences of commands, and you may wish to show these as lists of words or symbols. Once complete, ask the children to think about additional capabilities their robots have and ask them to create their own lists of sequences for others to follow with the robot.

Bonus idea ★

The verbal commands don't need to stop with the robots! In a game where the player moves around as a character, such as Minecraft, the teacher could ask the children en masse to carry out tasks verbally. This will probably not achieve much. Instead, ask the children to form pairs and have one of each pair operating the controls with the other as a 'backseat driver' telling the operator what to do.

#RubbishRobots

Coding cards

'I would like a fun active game to help my pupils work in sequences.'

Following sequences and still remembering past commands is difficult for humans. When coding, we sometimes forget to stop a command, and therefore it continues unchecked, which causes an issue. This next activity highlights the need to stop code or give an additional instruction to counter your original instruction.

Firstly, download the coding cards from the Online Resources and print enough so each child has a set or two. Explain to the class what each of the symbols means. I have made some suggestions for meanings on the coding cards sheets, but feel free to interpret these differently and add to the cards if you wish. You may even wish the children to put their own interpretation on the cards. Point out any cards which are similar and could be confused, such as the *spinning* and *repeating* cards. You can ask the children to write a note on the backs of the cards if you feel it may be needed.

In the school hall or other open space, ask the children to shuffle their cards and then look at the card on top and do that action. Once the action is completed, that card goes to the bottom of the pack and the next action is carried out. The important point here is that unless a card gives you a counter instruction, the command continues. So, if the first card is *pull a face*, the face must remain pulled until the smile card is seen. The same is true of the *forward* card. The children must keep moving forward until another movement card is seen.

The high five card is a special one. It requires two people to complete it. So, if no one is waiting for a high five, the pupil must wait with their hand up until someone else needs to high five, then they can travel over to give one.

Taking it further

Adapt a hopscotch floor pattern so each square has a command to do, e.g. pull a funny face, until overridden by another command, e.g. smile, as the player continues along the hopscotch track.

#CodingCards

13

Algorithms and instructions

Part 2

Beginning to scratch

'Where can I find an easy-to-use coding platform for children?'

There are thousands of programming languages in existence today, from JavaScript, which underpins much of the web and mobile phone applications, to COBOL, which lies at the heart of financial platforms and military infrastructure.

There are two main coding platforms that are used in school – Scratch and Python. Much of this book uses Scratch as it is an entry-level coding platform which uses colourful blocks, rather than lots of text, that can be bolted together to create simple games and applications.

Access Scratch through your web browser at **scratch.mit.edu**. Your pupils will need an account each, and these are free to sign up to. From the dashboard, users will see the '**Create**', '**Explore**' menu items as well as a search bar; these will be the main areas your pupils will use.

In the **Explore** section and the search bar, users can discover projects created by the community. Projects on Scratch can be remixed, meaning that you can make a copy of the project, see the code that underpins it, tinker with the code, and then republish it. Some of the best learning that happens on the platform is seeing how other people have solved problems or taking an existing project and improving it with your own coding knowledge.

Pressing **Create** takes you to your project editing page. This consists of a white square stage, which has the character of a cat in the centre of it as default. Below this are your sprites, which are your characters, objects and backdrops which interact on the stage.

In Scratch 3.0, at the top left of the screen you will find three tabs, '*Code*', '*Costume*' and '*Sounds*'.

Code is where you will spend most of your time, as it is where the coding happens. There are ten coloured sections where users can find blocks of code which can be dragged to the right onto the grey coding area. We will explore these coloured sections at length throughout this book, and you will notice that there are many coloured blocks under each coloured section. This grey area is unique to each sprite, and you will see that the code for each sprite will be different. At the bottom, on the coding blocks area, is the '*Add Extension*' button. There are additional '*Music*', '*Pen*' and '*Video motion*' blocks within, as well as speech recognition and many ways to use hardware, such as the Micro:bit and Lego™ devices with Scratch.

Many sprites have a few different forms, which allows you to animate their movements. These can be found under the *Costumes* tab. For example, the default cat has two different versions which make it look like it is walking.

The final section is the *Sounds* tab. This is where users can record or upload sounds to incorporate into your projects. Audio for projects is often forgotten about, and sounds bring an immersive element to your projects.

There is a lot to unpick here, and the only way to know it well is to explore it and use it. Try a few test projects from this book, follow some online tutorials, click and right-click on everything to see what it does, but most of all have fun!

Bonus idea ★

The library of projects from other Scratch users will be an invaluable resource while learning to use the platform. Not only can pupils copy individual blocks of code, they can duplicate an entire project to explore and tinker with the code.

#BeginScratch

Where to?

'The pupils find it difficult to navigate objects around the screen.'

Spatial awareness can be an issue for young children (and adults), but taking a different vantage point can help them move around in 3D space.

Many games and platforms use maps to convey information or allow the user to explore. Getting from A to B is fairly simple, but travelling from one position to any other destination offers additional challenges.

Make a model town using cardboard boxes, building blocks or a ready-made playmat with a town design. As space allows, ask groups to explore the town and identify five to eight landmarks. Ask the pupils to measure the distance, first in a straight line, then using roads, using standard units for older pupils or lengths of string for younger pupils. You can ask each group to do a few each and collate a table. Your pupils should find that using the roads gives longer distances than moving directly between two places. Ask the pupils to make symbolic or written instructions to travel between each location. Again, assign a few routes to each group and collate.

Either photograph a 'bird's eye view' of the town and import it or draw a town directly on Scratch, ensuring that there are a number of landmarks to navigate between. Using Scratch, ask the pupils to work out how to navigate between each using code. This may use coordinate, movement and/or direction blocks from the *Motion* section and either letter or picture triggers from the *Events* section. They will also need to design a vehicle. For less advanced pupils, use a circle for the vehicle so that turning isn't necessary. See an example in the Online Resources for this book.

#CodingWhere

Recipe for coding

'How can I practise algorithms in practical parts of the curriculum?'

Cooking apps are very popular these days. These give detailed instructions for budding chefs to get their recipes and cooking just right.

Ask your pupils to create a recipe project using Scratch. There are many ways they might tackle this. Probably the easiest way to create slides is by designing backdrops using the paintbrush tool. Add all the pictures, text and any other items you wish to add as part of the one image so they do not need to be coded individually.

Add some sprites to act as buttons to link to each numbered slide (use the numbers available from the sprite library for ease). To each of the numbered button sprites, add the script *when this sprite clicked* from the *Events* section as a trigger. From the *Looks* section, add *switch to backdrop_____* and select the particular backdrop which you want to link that number to.

Use the green flag above your stage as a reset of the recipe. Use the *when green flag clicked* block from the *Events* section as a trigger and then add the code to make everything appear as it did at the beginning of the recipe project.

To go to the next level, use exactly the same code to design a project where users can select from a list of meals. Pupils could even create a project based on the choice of school meals for a day or a week.

See a basic example in the Online Resources for this book.

Taking it further

Use the *wait* block from the *Control* section to add recipe timings to automatically move the backdrop slide forward once the chef should move on, and use this to signal cooking times.

#RecipeCode

Building code

'How can I create a simple set of instructions for building models?'

Paper-based instructions can be complex and difficult to follow. Sometimes it's difficult to see what is happening. Create a numbered set of instructions using text and uploaded images.

In small groups, ask your pupils to decide on a simple model to make, e.g. a paper aeroplane or a Lego™ car. To keep things simple, ask them not to exceed four steps. Next, they will need to think carefully about which step they want to show and write very brief instructions for each of these. The groups should attempt to build their model several times using these instructions only, ensuring that they make sense. Take up to four photos of the model at key moments in its construction to help a would-be builder understand what they must do at that stage.

Using Scratch, upload the four photos as sprites. Create four more sprites using the *Choose a sprite* button. Type the instruction text for the four chosen stages into the individual sprites. Next, choose number sprites from the sprite library within Scratch, again using the *Choose a sprite* button. Arrange the numbers down one side of the stage, numbering 1 to 4 in order.

Using the *script when this sprite clicked* from the *Events* section as a trigger for each of the numbers, connect the appropriate *broadcast____* from the *Events* section so the numbers can signal to other sprites. Use the *when I receive____* block from the *Events* section to trigger showing or hiding the text and image. Connect the *hide* or *show* blocks from the *Looks* section for each photo text. The code for the photo and its corresponding text should be displayed at exactly the same.

#BuildingCode

Teatime

'How can I create something which is useful to the staff?'

There are many important things which make schools run effectively — good communication, staff and pupil wellbeing, and creative ideas. But there is one thing which should be prized above all else for making a school run smoothly — tea and coffee!

Ask your pupils to design a system for the staffroom which helps a user look up and make the perfect tea or coffee for a particular member of staff. Take photos of the staff to be included. Three or four will be fine for this prototype. Using Scratch, add the photos to the project as sprites.

Write the tea or coffee instructions for each person on a backdrop, e.g. 'white, no sugar'. Pupils should also add a backdrop as a title page to show user instructions for how to use the tea/coffee assistant.

Using the script **when this sprite clicked** from the *Events* section as a trigger for each of the photos, connect a **broadcast____** from the *Events* section with the name of the person in the blank space. This will signal to the backdrop to change. For each of the four tea/coffee instruction backdrops, use the **when I receive____** block from the *Events* section to trigger showing the staff member's image and hiding the others, while also changing the backdrop to the appropriate one. Use the **hide** or **show** blocks from the *Looks* section for each photo. Add the **when green flag clicked** trigger from *Events* as a reset and return to the title page, ensuring that all staff photos return and only the instructions about how to use the tea/coffee assistant are shown.

See the example in the Online Resources.

Taking it further

Create a similar project which profiles each child in the class in a table. Include details like birth month, likes and dislikes, pet names, etc. Each piece of information could appear independently, so the user could see, e.g. only the birth month and nothing else.

#TeaTimeCode

Weather forecast

'How can I use coding to create backdrops for filming videos of my pupils?'

Coding weather sequence map animations is a great way to bring a real-world application to your classroom and bring lots of coding techniques together. The weather is notoriously unpredictable, but perhaps your pupils can bring some order to this chaos through coding.

Taking it further

In addition, your pupils can design an animated speaking weather presenter using recorded audio to be played automatically or *say* text block from the *Looks* section.

Watch a clip of a weather forecast with your pupils and note the symbols being used and the types of things which are discussed.

On Scratch, import or draw a map for the backdrop. Import or draw the weather symbols and temperature numbers for the weather report. Ensure that these are independent sprites which can move individually. Ask your pupils to design a backdrop costume as a title page, which should include the names of the presenters. To switch between costumes, add a trigger, such as *when space key pressed,* and use the costume blocks in the *Looks* section.

Place the weather symbols onto the map and code each to *glide__sec to x:__ y:__* coordinates with the trigger as key '1' on your keyboard. Repeat in slightly different locations and/or hide and show symbols using key '2' as a trigger, and so on until you have built up an animated sequence.

The pupils can add in days and times to make the animation more authentic. For advanced coders, you can request that they use automatic timings using the *wait* function. They may even wish to use the camera to operate the animation from the *Video motion* extension section, followed by *video___on___*.

#CodingWeather

Code hunt

'I want to practise making and following sequences while engaged in outdoor learning.'

Instructions are not something you can only learn in the classroom. Instructions and sequences are all around us, where one piece of information leads you to the next.

QR (quick reference) codes are 2D barcodes which are popular in Asia, but they are greatly underused in the UK, especially in education. These allow you to encode information such as text, website links and much more for a digital device to read quickly and without the need for an Internet connection. There are many apps and websites where you can create QR codes.

QRExplore at *qrexplore.com* is just one example. Create a scavenger hunt by writing clues and/or instructions and then encoding them in QR codes. Each clue will lead the hunters to the next. Using a QR code reader, ask your pupils to complete the treasure hunt.

Next, ask the pupils to create their own QR code treasure hunt. Firstly, they will need to think about the instructions they want to give and put these into a logical order, just like creating an algorithm. When positioning the QR codes, they need to find a good balance between making the treasure hunters use the clues, and therefore making them less obvious, and hiding them so well that they will never be found. The treasure hunt creators should try out their own hunt and have a chance to debug if necessary. If many groups are deploying QR codes at the same time, ensure that they can be distinguished by adding colours or labels.

Bonus idea ★

QR codes have so many different uses in the classroom: stick them on the covers of workbooks to allow parents to access their child's blog page; add them to displays to make them interactive; or create an online reading record by asking parents to scan a QR code which links to a Google Form, meaning the record is always to hand for both teacher and parent.

#CodeHunt

Shape drawing

'How can I use coding to explore 2D shapes in my class?'

In my own primary school days, I spent many happy hours watching a triangular turtle not move very much. Games have evolved unimaginably since the MSWLogo first became available, but coaxing a turtle to do your bidding still has benefits when it comes to learning coding.

Teaching tip

Explore 2D shapes in the real world first. Take some coloured electrical tape and create shapes on the floor and then measure the lengths and angles before drawing in the virtual world.

Taking it further

Ask your coders to explore repeating geometric shapes which are reminiscent of a Spirograph™ pattern using the *forever* block from the *Control* section and very acute vertices. Change the colour of the pen by using the *set pen color to___* block from the *Pen* section.

#ShapeCode

Your class are no doubt well versed in talking about vertices, edges and faces of shapes from their maths lessons. Ask them to use this knowledge to draw 2D shapes in Scratch. Firstly, your pupils will need to explore the movement blocks in the *Motion* section, which will allow them to turn and move forward. They will also need to use the *repeat___* C-shaped block from the *Control* section to allow them to repeat the same movement to create the same angles and forward movements more easily.

Ask your pupils to choose an appropriate sprite, e.g. a pencil, from the sprite library. They may also wish to shrink this to make the drawing easier to see using the resizing tools at the top of the screen. Ask your pupils to use a trigger such as the green flag. Using the *pen down* block from the *Pen* extension section, ask them to use turns and the *forward___* block to create a square. Adapt the code to draw other regular shapes like triangles, heptagons, hexagons and so on.

Next, ask the pupils to draw the more challenging irregular shapes, such as rectangles or stars.

Checklists

'How can my class create checklists to remind them to do things around the class?'

As a teacher, I love lists – despite my to-do list expanding exponentially. Lists keep us organised, which is something that many of our pupils need to work on.

Firstly, your pupils need to think about what their list is going to be about. This will change the format of the list. For example, a checklist may need tick boxes along the side to show what has been done, whereas a to-do list will need some way to add items and to remove them once completed. For the latter, use the *make a list* function within the *Variables* section in Scratch.

For a checklist, which will be used again and again, it's important to have some way of indicating which tasks on the list have been completed. As the list will remain static, add the items you want on your list directly onto a backdrop, as these will probably remain on the stage all of the time.

Either from the sprite library, drawing them by hand, or by searching and then uploading, find images of a tick and a cross. Create a sprite with two costumes: a tick and a cross. Put a version of the sprite next to each of the statements. Use the *when this sprite clicked* block from *Events* and the *next costume* block from *Looks* to make the sprite change from a cross to a tick once the item has been completed.

Create checklists for writing stories, a self-marking list so your pupils can check for more mistakes before coming to you and, most importantly, what to remember when you are coding.

#Checklists

Coding parents

'How can my pupils use coding to create a smooth parents' evening ... is that possible?'

Watching parents' evenings in many different schools gives you a sense of both how similar and how different schools can be. Each school has to deliver a similar event, but each has its own traditions, needs and routines.

Firstly, choose an issue you want your pupils to tackle. It could be a meet-and-greet interface, an interface for parents to show that they have arrived or a checklist for parents to use to ensure that they make the most of their time at the school.

You could use Scratch to create a system to log which parents have arrived. First, you will need to list all of the children's names within a class and show these to parents. If this includes surnames, do not share these online. The parents then click on their child's name and the name disappears and is replaced by the appointment time and/or what to do next, e.g. browse their child's books. Your coders can achieve this by adding each name as a text sprite and using the *when this sprite clicked* block from the *Events* section and moving to the next costume which shows the additional information, using the *next costume* block from *Looks*.

You could use the same system to create a series of stations for parents to go to so that you can create an algorithm of parental instructions. For example, once the computer at the entrance has been clicked, it tells parents to go and look at the class's work on a display. The computer at the display will invite parents to browse their child's work in their tray when clicked, and so on.

#CodingParents

Flow charts

'I would like to explore flow charts using algorithms.'

Flow charts are a staple of computer science because they aid the thinking of complex processes, which may have many twists and turns. Let's design a project which creates an interactive flow chart.

Ask your class to create a decision list of all the choices they made during an entire average school day from the moment they got up to when they went to bed. The next day, collate the lists together as a class and pick out some of the more common items which appear on many people's list. Some of these will include what activities to do during downtime and break times, as well as mealtime choices.

In small groups, ask your pupils to combine their common elements, up to four decisions, which actually change the course of their day. While it is not a choice but a variable, going or not going to school seems like a clear divergence within their day, and this might make a good first decision. Because the flow chart is meant to be for making decisions and seeing the consequences, keep the language in future tense.

In Scratch, use the *when this sprite clicked* block from the *Events* section to create yes or no clickable text sprites to a question like 'Are you going to school today?' which change the backdrop to the next question. This will eventually show the collective consequences of all of the decisions. In the unlikely event that your pupils think it was a bad decision not to go to school after they had clicked and chosen not to, add a clickable back button to take the user back one step.

> **Bonus idea** ★
>
> Use a virtual flow chart to map out possible plot scenarios for stories and creative writing as part of the planning process.

#FlowCoding

Problem solving
and debugging

Part 3

Teacherbot

'Teaching is a rewarding but difficult profession. Sometimes I would like a bit of help.'

It's always nice to have a little assistance in the classroom. Let your pupils design some for you.

Firstly, your pupils will need to think about a teacher's key attributes. Don't be offended – this may yield some interesting insights! Ask your pupils to focus on a particular lesson, perhaps one which you have taught recently, so they have the required prior knowledge, or you could ask your pupils to conduct research for a future lesson. They will then design the lesson using Scratch.

Because a large amount of what a teacher does involves his or her voice, adding speech will be an important aspect of this activity. Pupils can do this via the **Looks** tab and use the **say** blocks, or they can use audio via the **Sound** tab and **play sound** blocks.

Just like a real dynamic classroom, they can create sprites to interact with the user, displays using different backdrop costumes, and a variety of triggers, such as using keyboard keys to begin a range of actions. Your pupils may like to create a user guide separately to keep track of which keys prompt which actions.

Questioning is an important part of teaching, and your pupils should include this aspect of the classroom in their virtual teaching resource. From the **Sensing** tab, choose **ask___and wait**. In this block, you can ask your question. You can see a simple example in the Online Resources if you find the instructions on the next page tricky to follow.

So that the computer knows whether the answer is correct, you need to use some logic.

Under your question block, use an *if__then__ else* block from the *Control* tab; the block looks like a capital 'E'. In between the 'if' and 'then' you need to use some maths to share which answer is correct. Use the ___=___ block from the *Operators* tab together with the *answer* block from the *Sensing* tab. In the top gap of the capital E, the *then* space, you can add what you want to happen if the question is answered correctly, and in the lower *else* space, you can add the condition for when the user gets the question wrong. This can be text or audio feedback or a change of backdrop, or you could even use a variable to include a score.

Allow your pupils time to try out and assess the bots created by other groups and to add additional features where necessary.

Finally, attempt to teach a mini-lesson for a few minutes using the bot. Ask the children to comment on which commands might have been useful in retrospect.

#Teacherbot

Hacking the Web

'How can I show my class how web coding skills can be used?'

Hacking gets a rap. It's true — criminals exploit vulnerabilities to gain access to restricted information and compromise systems. But more accurately, hacking means to tinker with something or repurpose it for something for which it was not originally intended.

Most web developers would be uncomfortable handing over the keys to their sites and allowing others to play and poke at the code. But the tools at *goggles.mozilla.org* allow you to make a copy of most webpages and change the code to see what it does.

Go to the Goggles site and follow the instructions to drag the bookmarklet to your bookmark bar. You will need to do this on every computer the pupils will use, and there may be network restrictions on this.

Design a comical website story using the techniques in this idea. Perhaps it could be news of your Teacher of the Year Award that you've been very quiet about, or 'headteacher bites man'. Show this to the pupils and see what their reaction is. A few of your pupils should begin to question the authenticity of the story (Teacher of the Year? You?). Once that happens, talk to them about how you've edited the site and changed the text and images. This could lead on to a wider conversation about the trustworthiness of articles and posts that can be found on the Web.

Ask your pupils to navigate to a safe page, such as *bbc.co.uk/newsround*, and click on the bookmark. They should now notice that when they hover over different elements of the web page, these elements are highlighted in different colours. Ask them to click on a piece of text; they should see an editing panel at the bottom of the screen. This is the HTML code for that piece of text. Somewhere in the editing panel will be the exact same text as appears on the web page. Ask pupils to try changing the text to something else. Once they are happy with their edits, press the *Update* button to save the text.

Next, pupils should choose an image in the same way. They will see the filename and the address of where the image is stored online, usually ending in .jpg or .png. Pupils should search for a replacement image using your search engine of choice. They need to aim for an image of a similar shape so it fits well into the page. Pupils should on *View Image* to see the image in isolation, which should give the web address of where this image is stored in the address bar. Pupils should copy and paste this web address into the Goggles editing window, press *Update*, and they should see the image has changed. For hyperlinks on text or images, videos or audio media, pupils should be able to change the link location in a similar way.

Once complete, pupils can click *Publish* and share the altered page with whomever you wish using the generated link.

The important part of this activity is to poke and tinker to see what is possible and discover how it can be achieved.

Bonus idea ★

Use the Goggles bookmarklet to create stimulus for your lessons. Whether it's a history lesson about sources, a creative writing lesson which has a new story at its heart, a computing lesson where you are focusing on fake news, trusted gatekeepers and website reliability, or simply altering a website to remove unsuitable content to use in your lessons, being able to edit websites to make them useful in your classroom has many advantages.

#HackingCode

Debugging fish

'How can my class practise debugging when they cannot find their own mistakes?'

Designing one's own program is one thing; you have an understanding of the thinking behind the code and it should make logical sense, at least to you. Debugging other people's work can be a lot more complicated because you must first understand the thinking behind the coding before you can begin to fix problems.

Ask your class about glitches within the games they have played. They will likely tell you about characters walking through walls, sprites with no heads and characters getting stuck in invisible treacle. Considering how complex modern gaming is, it's amazing that there are not more glitches.

In Scratch, ask the pupils to explore the 'Debug fish' game (a link is available in the Online Resources). The game isn't working as it should, and there is a consistent error in the code which your pupils need to discover and fix. (Shhhhh – between you and me, the clickable numbers along the top all set the shark to strength nine and therefore the shark will overshoot every time.)

Once the children have discovered the issue, ask them to indulge their destructive tendencies and to search for a fairly simple game, make a remix copy of it, break it in a small way and share it with their peers to practise debugging and fixing problems. If they are feeling confident, they could even search for games which they feel could use a little more work and improve them.

#DebuggingFish

Sorting it out

'I want to create something which will sort objects and identify them by their properties.'

Computers and other digital devices have had an exponential growth in use in business commerce and in almost every other aspect of life. One thing that artificial intelligence is helping machines to do with greater accuracy is identify real-world objects and sort them, especially in the field of logistics.

Create a sorting project, where asking questions will lead to the code identifying the right object. This could be clothes, cars, people or, as in the 'Coin coding' example in the Online Resources, used to identify coins.

Take photos or source images from a web search. Upload these into Scratch. Use Y and N sprites from the sprite library to answer 'yes' or 'no' to each answer. Write the questions directly on the backdrops. These will be switched as each question is answered.

Using the block *when this sprite clicked* from the *Events* section as a trigger for the Y or N sprites, connect a *broadcast____* block from the *Events* section with the condition for your answers (for the coin example, *silver Y* or *silver N*). This will signal the backdrop to change. For each of the questions, you will need a different set of Y and N sprites to allow a click to work for different questions. Change the backdrops by using the *when I receive____* block from the *Events* section to trigger hiding the coins which are not right and keeping the coins which might still be right at this stage. Use the *hide* block from the *Looks* section to make the appropriate coins disappear. Add the *when green flag clicked* trigger from *Events* as a reset and return to the title page, ensuring that all the coins and Y/N sprites are showing or hidden as needed.

Teaching tip

Lots of changes will happen in sequence, which may be a little difficult to track. Ask your pupils to note down on paper when each object should disappear to help keep track of them.

#SortingOut

Battle bots

'My pupils are becoming great coders, but now they want to make two-player games that interact with other objects.'

Games are dynamic. The best games allow one sprite to interact with another. Shooter games are a great example of this.

Taking it further

Ouch! Make the bot sense the impact of projectiles by using blocks from the *Sensing* section. An easy way to do this is by using colours. Make your bots different colours and when your projectile touches, say red, you can increase the points or go to a 'Game Over' screen.

In Scratch, design a sprite to be your battle bot. A circle or rectangle will suffice. Use arrow trigger keys from the *Events* section to allow your bot to navigate backwards and forwards, and also turn clockwise and anticlockwise. Duplicate the bot and make the second bot look different in some way using *Costumes*. Review the script of the second bot and change the keys used to navigate.

Choose or design a projectile sprite and ask your pupils to experiment with the *point in direction___* block to allow a projectile to move away from the firing sprite in the direction it is currently facing. Naturally, the projectile should appear to be emerging from the bot, so use the *go to___* block from the *Motion* tab to make the projectile begin firing at the other bot.

Because you are really firing the same projectile again and again, your pupils should use the *hide* and *show* block from *Looks* to give the illusion that different projectiles are being fired.

Your pupils may wish to halt the projectile at the edge of the page or allow it to bounce – find the former in the *Sensing* tab and the latter in the *Motion* tab. See the 'Bots battle' example in the Online Resources. Scratch games can be remixed, so your pupils can copy other pupils' creations into their own stages and pit one sprite against another. The class can create a battle league – only the strongest will survive!

#BattleBots

Class app

'I want my class to build an app to keep parents up to date with what we are doing.'

There is an app for everything these days, from news, social and fitness apps to educational and games apps. But using them to improve communication between home and school should be of great interest to any teacher.

Design a web app for your class. There are many different platforms which you could use to achieve this, with *appinventor.mit.edu* and *appshed.com* being just two dedicated app-building websites, and you can also use Scratch if you wish.

There are three main stages to building an app. Firstly, your pupils will need to research what the class and teacher want to communicate to the wider world. Take a look at the school's website and talk about what is good about it and what your pupils feel could be improved. Discuss eSafety and stress that whenever somebody posts online, they should be wary about giving out personal details. Talk about the things which can and can't be posted.

Ask your pupils to do research with the app's audience – their parents. The needs of the audience may not be the same as those of the school, and this should be talked about in class.

The second stage is the actual design and building of the app. Most online app builders use drag and drop tools, which are fairly straightforward, and your pupils can use their existing skills and knowledge to build their app using Scratch, if you have chosen this option.

The final stage is testing, debugging and making changes based on feedback from the users. Just like real apps, updates and improvements mean that an app is never truly finished.

Taking it further

Create an app to solve problems and aid learning in class. This can be an app which helps pupils learn times tables or a digital homework diary.

#ClassApp

Teacher's pet

'My pupils seem to only use static characters in their games.'

Not every classroom is lucky enough to have a class pet. There's no reason why your pupils can't create an interactive virtual pet.

Taking it further

To extend the activity, you can add speech bubbles so the pet can express its needs via the **Looks** tab. To extend it even further you can add a health score using the **make a variable** block from the **Variables** tab which decreases by 1 point after an allotted time but is reset to 100% when you interact with the pet.

Building a virtual pet will use a range of different pieces of code, including changing the appearance of your pet, clicking on objects to move towards them and animating them.

Your pupils will need to think about what kind of creature their pet will be and which objects the pet will need in its surroundings.

In Scratch, add a suitable backdrop to the creature's enclosure and lock that layer in place. Add or draw objects like a sleeping basket, a bowl, a water bottle and some entertainment as individual sprites. Use the **when sprite is clicked** and the **broadcast____** blocks to initiate actions when the objects are clicked.

Add the **when I receive____** block to your pet sprite and code a **glide__secs to x:__ y:__** block to make the pet move to that object.

Once the pet is at the object, you can create a costume to change the appearance of the pet so it looks like it is interacting with the object, for example, eating at the food bowl. This is done using the **switch costume to____** block. For the best results, it's good to alternate between two costumes using a **wait__secs** block in between. You can also animate the objects in the same way.

Lastly, automatically reset the scene after each interaction by returning the pet to the middle of the screen using the **glide__secs to x:__ y:__** block. See the example virtual pet in the Online Resources.

#TeachersPet

38

Composition code

'How can I teach coding using our class blog?'

Blogging as a class is a superbly educational and satisfying pursuit. Class blogs are amazing for providing a real audience for your pupils' creativity, and are a wonderful way to engage with parents. But you can also use a blog to learn about coding.

Firstly, a disclaimer: blogs usually use HTML to create a blog post, and professional programmers would say that it's a markup language rather than a programming language, but I think it's fine for our umbrella term of 'code'.

Most blogs have two modes for writing and editing blogs for users – visual editing (sometimes called WYSIWYG, pronounced wiz-ee-wig, meaning 'what you see is what you get') and text editing. It's the latter which is of interest to us.

Ask your pupils to create a new post in the visual composer and then to add a little text with some formatting and also an image. On the same post, move over to the text composer and you will see the same post coded in HTML. Look for the link to the image you added and replace it with a new one you find via a search engine.

Ask your pupils to change the text into bold by putting ** at the beginning of the section and ** at the end. If you switch back to the visual editor, you should see that the text in between these has become bold.

Try ** and ** to use italics for emphasis and *<li>* and *</li>* for a list of bullet points. There are many longer HTML strings, like *Replace * to change the colour of the text to red, for example. Discover more at *www.html.am*.

> **Teaching tip**
>
> Got a class blog with a single username? Explore 'roles' to allow your pupils to have their own accounts; they can submit posts but these will remain hidden until you choose to publish them.

#BlogCode

Clock conundrums

'How can my class create a clock using coding?'

While it is possible to create an analogue clock using coding and calculate the correct angles of the hands, computers work best with numbers. As such, creating a digital display is an order of magnitude easier.

Taking it further

Now that you have your clock, your pupils will need to figure out a way to set it, as it is not always practical to start it at midnight – the site manager will complain! Create clickable arrows in combination with the *switch costume to___* block from the *Looks* section.

Firstly, ask your pupils to experiment in Scratch and create a countdown from 10 to 0 using sprites for the numbers. The double digits of '10' may cause them to think carefully about how to code for this. One way is to use the *broadcast___* and *when I receive___* blocks from the *Events* section to signal to both digits to hide at the same time. They could also code both numbers to hide one after the other and then use a *wait* block in between making them hide almost simultaneously. Use the *wait___secs* block from the *Control* section to insert a one second gap in between each of the numbers in the countdown.

Using the skills and knowledge from the above activity, ask your pupils to create a working digital clock with six digits in total (hours, minutes and seconds). Instead of having double-digit numbers made from two sprites, they can design 60 different sprites for each of the double-digit minutes. To make the coding easier, your pupils can combine each of the double digits as a costume in one sprite and simply use the next costume block from the *Looks* section. Rather than creating three double-digit sprites, your pupils can create one with up to 60 costumes and then copy it by right-clicking on the sprite and adapting it if necessary.

#ClockConundrums

Thank you, Alexa

'Can we create a digital assistant like Alexa or Siri?'

Speaking digital assistants are becoming more commonplace in people's homes, but are still relatively rare in the classroom. With this next idea, this could be about to change.

Using Scratch, ask your class to think about some very common enquiries that people may ask their digital assistants. Your pupils may wish for the user to input their queries as text or simply click on a button. Below, I will explain how to make the latter, but you can adapt this to typing by using the *ask____ and wait* block and the *answer* block from the *Sensing* section.

You should allow the pupils to attempt to solve this for themselves in their own way. There are a number of ways this can be achieved, and below is just one example.

Ask your pupils to decide on four questions and think of the answers. Create four text sprites by using the paintbrush tool. Use the script *when this sprite clicked* from the *Events* section as a trigger for each of the text sprites.

Next, click on the *Sounds* tab above the coloured block sections. Upload or record the questions and answers to each one, with the questions as audio. Once recorded, use the *play sound_____* block from the coloured *Sound* section of the *Code* tab. Also add a brief *wait__ secs*. Use this to first read out the question, pause briefly, and then read out the answer.

Ask pupils from another group to test the prototype and debug where necessary.

Bonus idea

Using a similar method, you could make a knowledge bank as an end-of-topic summary for future pupils to use. Instead of simply clicking on text questions, the user could click on maps, images or buttons to discover more about the topic.

#CodingAlexa

Scrolling

'How can I scroll the screen in Scratch, as the screen is very small?'

Want to scroll the screen? Don't, unless you really have to. It's a tricky thing to get right with only basic coding skills, so use a few tricks instead to cheat.

When I'm covering this aspect of building a project, I try to allow my pupils to explore and figure out workarounds. In the past, my pupils have thought of ideas I would never have had – this is problem solving at its best. However, when covering this in class, it's important that the teacher appears knowledgeable, so look at my example of one solution in the Online Resources. I have offset the images so you can see what is happening. Essentially, there are two images which appear on one side, slide across the screen when the user presses the arrow keys, and then another image comes in behind them to hide the white backdrop before the first image disappears. It's the same principle as when you create a never-ending bridge for a walking hamster with your hands.

Another trick is to not move things in the background at all, but to move things in the foreground which give the illusion of movement. See my '3D road race' example in the Online Resources. In this project, the road is a rectangle which continually wobbles and moves left and right. There are also trees moving upwards on the stage, giving the sense that the whole background is moving that way, but the green background isn't moving at all.

Teaching tip

See Idea 35 in the following section for an additional technique.

Bonus idea ★

Create a scrolling photo. Take a series of photos moving left or right parallel to the object of interest, perhaps a group photo of the class close enough so not everyone can fit in the frame. Use scrolling techniques to allow a user to virtually move along the image sequence giving the effect of a continuous long image.

#ScrollingCode

Designing games and animation

Part 4

3D games

'My pupils want to design 3D games like they see on their consoles at home.'

Most modern blockbuster games have teams of people working on them, but you can go some way to making simple 2D games look a little more 3D. There are also game engines which allow you to build 3D environments.

#3DGames

The easiest way to make a 2D platform look more 3D is by introducing perspective. See a simple example of this in the Online Resources for this book. In this example the road is angled so there is an illusion that the road at the bottom of the page is closer to the user. The trees moving past help to create the illusion as well. See '3D Action' and '3D Rain' in the Online Resources for two more great examples.

Scratch allows users to copy and remix projects. Ask your pupils to research interesting 3D designs uploaded to Scratch by other users, including looking at the code and examining how it works. They should try changing the numbers and blocks of the coding to see what happens.

Next, ask your pupils to design their own 3D projects in groups of two or three, using elements of other projects from remixes and adding snippets of code.

Once your pupils have completed their designs, allow other groups to try the game and offer suggestions for improvements. Allow the original group to make corrections if needed.

A change of scene

'I want the background of our games to change as the character moves off scene.'

As was stated in Idea 33 in the previous section, true scrolling is tricky with only a basic knowledge of coding. Early platforms, such as the early Mario games or *Flappy Bird*, had static backgrounds, and it was only the foreground objects which moved. Scrolling a background for the entire level requires one long graphic which slowly slides across the screen.

Another pleasing technique to work around the issue of scrolling in Scratch is to have individual scenes so when your character walks off the page they appear on the far side of the scene, as if they've just entered, and the background will have changed. See my example of this in the Online Resources.

Firstly, the sprite character must be given some way to move. My example uses the *if* block from the *Control* section and screen coordinates to say that if the sprite reaches a certain point, it will be transported to the opposite side of the screen and the backdrop will change. If you don't want to use coordinates, you can get a similar effect by using the *if* block with a *touching color___?* block from the *Sensing* section and add a thin link for the triggering colour down the very edge of the screen.

It is important that this works on both sides of the screen and that the code can be copied and adapted to the other side easily.

Taking it further

Adventure games often base the environment on a series of rooms, and the player appears to be looking down at the floor over their character; the classic Zelda games are examples of this. You can design a game where the character walks off screen in one of four possible directions and there is a different scene waiting. This quickly expands the gaming area to as many squares as you wish. Don't want your character to go any further? Draw a wall and delete the code for that direction for that backdrop.

#ChangeScene

Animated sequences

'I want to animate our game's title page.'

Animation is absolutely vital in game design. It's how characters move, it's how scenery appears to change, and it's integral to the gameplay. There are also a myriad of different ways in which to do it.

There are two main sections of Scratch that are useful in animation – *Motion* and *Looks*. We have explored both of these in many of the earlier ideas in this book. As we are designing a title sequence, we could begin with some storyline where we animate sprite characters and set up the story for the game.

In the example in the Online Resources, I have designed a simple menu with option selection. The cursor moves up and down as the arrow keys are pressed. This uses a variable, a number which changes depending of the conditions set by the code. Make a new variable from the *Variables* section. I have combined this with *if else* statement blocks from the *Control* section, mathematical blocks from the *Operators* section and coordinates blocks from the *Motion* section. These combine to say that if the variable is a given number, the cat sprite will be at those coordinates.

Of course, your animation doesn't necessarily need to be interactive at all and can simply be decoration on the page. Use *Forever* blocks from the *Control* section to keep your animations repeating without stopping.

Bonus idea ★

Scratch is an easy platform on which to practise animations, but not so accessible for watching them. You can export your animations as files of up to 60 seconds of video by going to *File*, then *Record & Export Video*. There are many options, including audio preferences and whether you want to record from your microphone.

#AnimatedSeq

Keeping score

'How do I make a scoring game using code?'

Scoring is essential in many games and brings a competitive element to a game. Yet, a scoring system is often an afterthought in pupil projects.

Scores, at the most basic level, are numbers which change when something happens. In Scratch, ask your pupils to design a simple game with a scoring system where two sprites touch to score a point. This could be a ball and a goal, a golf ball and a hole or a chasing game like the example in the Online Resources.

To keep a score you will need to use a variable, a number which changes as a result of some kind of interaction. As in the example, use the *touching___?* block from the *Sensing* tab. Set this to activate when touching another sprite. Add a trigger and some kind of response, such as 'well done' text.

Go to the *Variables* section and click *Make a Variable*. Give this the name of 'Score' and always keep variables assigned to all sprites unless there is a good reason not to do so. Once 'OK' has been clicked, you should see that a score has been added to the stage and more blocks have appeared on the *Variables* section. Now simply add your sensing blocks to the *Change score by___* to change the score each time the sprites touch.

Note that the score will continue to increase all the time that the sprites are touching, so if you want only one touch to increase the score by one, you may wish to reset the positions of the sprite(s) so they are separated straight after they touch for the first time.

Bonus idea ★

You can add the score variable into your code as a number so you can use it to create power-ups. As the score increases, you can change the size, speed or colour of a sprite.

#KeepingScore

Down-to-earth games

'I want my sprites to fall back down to Earth after they have jumped into the air.'

Gravity is something we rarely think about in our daily lives, but simulating gravity is a little tricky in games. Many games simply always drag the characters down, but the floor stops them from moving that way. When there is nothing under them, the characters move downwards at a constant rate and fall.

You can simulate accelerated falling in Scratch by using a variable which increases or decreases with the intended velocity of movement. See my example in the Online Resources. Hit the spacebar to see the ball jump. You should notice that the jump is fast at first, but as gravity begins to pull, the speed decreases until the sprite begins to fall again. Use this project as a template or example to build platform games with gravity.

Firstly, ensure that the direction of your sprite is straight up. Check this by clicking on the information *i* on the sprite in the sprite window. There are many other options to explore, but you need to turn the direction dial to 'up' or '0°'.

This example project uses a *touching color___?* and a black rectangle as a floor to stop any motion as the ball hits the ground. This sets the velocity to zero.

The jump and fall are created by setting the gravity variable to −10 so the ball is pushed into the air. At the same time, the variable is increasing each second. When it briefly reaches zero, the ball will be at its pinnacle and the number will continue to increase and bring the ball down faster and faster until it hits the black floor.

Ask the children to explore what changing each of the variables does and incorporate their discoveries into their own games.

#CodeGravity

Screen jump

'I want to sync my animations on multiple screens so characters and actions can interact on different screens.'

One screen not enough? Putting together a cartoon where the characters move to adjacent screens, just like the paintings in Harry Potter, is a wonderful effect and is fairly simple to do. It just takes timing.

See the example of a screen jumping animation in the Online Resources. You don't have to dance around with your devices like in the video. You can simply line them up on a table or even have your characters jumping from screen to screen in a computer suite.

Begin by asking your pupils to work in small groups to think of a storyline and to create a storyboard. At this time they should have access to two computers with Scratch to explore what is possible and how they can use the *wait___secs* block from the *Control* section to coordinate the animation. They may wish to create a timeline for each screen they wish to use it. Just like in the example video, the animation on each screen will need to begin at the same time to ensure everything is in sync. The group needs to think about how that can be done.

When the group is building the project, they will likely need to debug the timings repeatedly to get them right. They may benefit from having a stopwatch to refer to.

Once the videos are complete, your pupils may like to export their animations as videos to play on different devices. In some versions of Scratch, you can do this by going to *File*, then *Record & Export Video*.

> **Bonus idea** ★
>
> Create multiscreen animated educational presentations which interact with a person acting along with a script to bring together the digital and real world. To keep the relative scales similar, try using a large screen, such as the classroom whiteboard or a projector and screen in your hall if you have one.

#JumpScreen

You shall not pass

'How can we stop our characters walking through walls?'

Making characters walk *on* things, not through walls, and interact with things which are essentially just drawings means that the sprite needs to sense something about the barrier and for code to be triggered as a result.

Start a class discussion about how objects in games have no real substance and that code is needed to state that a character cannot move through a solid object. Explain that the same is true in Scratch, and ask your pupils if they can think of a way for objects to 'know' they are passing through something else. Show them my example of two spheres falling (available in the Online Resources). One sphere interacts with the red line, while the other interacts with the blue floor line. Both are using the *if else* E-shaped block from the *Control* section. They are coded to fall unless they are touching a specific colour. The blue ball is coded to travel at −128 degrees relative to the top of the page, which is the same angle as the red line. The other sphere stops all previous code when it is touching blue and therefore comes to a halt on the blue floor.

The colour which the sprite is sensitive to can be set in the *Sensing* section. Also, rather than the whole sprite being sensitive, you can set it up for the code to react when one chosen colour touches another specific colour.

You can get a similar effect using the *if else* block with coordinate conditions from the *Motion* section.

Bonus idea ★

Use the sensing of colour to create buzz loop games where the player must move between two forbidden lines without touching them. If there are touches the player must start again.

#ShallNotPass

Drawing platforms

'How can I design a game based on drawing.'

In Idea 40, we covered ways in which sprites can be made sensitive to colours and activate strings of code as a result. But colours and conditions don't just change in the editing process — they can change during the game too.

In Scratch, ask your pupils to explore the *Pen* extension section and try to put some of the block together with triggers to see what happens. They should find that the *pen up* block stops drawing while *pen down* allows it.

Find the ball sprite from the library and add it to the project. Make it much smaller using the shrink button near the top of the screen so it's only just invisible and so it doesn't obstruct the view of the background canvas. Use the *go to* mouse-pointer block from the *Motion* section to ensure that the ball sprite is always positioned at the mouse cursor. Using the *when___key pressed* block, choose one keyboard key to activate a *pen up* block and another to activate a *pen down* block. You should now be able to draw lines in the viewer mode by using these keys and the mouse.

Create a game where on-screen buttons allow you to activate a pen block for a limited time. These buttons should also change the colour of the pen. Make a sprite sensitive to one colour for 5 seconds in rotation using the *wait___secs* block from the *Control* section. Add some controls to allow the sprite to jump and move left and right, but ensure it's slowly moving all the time. The player will need to draw one of three coloured platforms quickly and try to jump to the top of the screen before the sprite doesn't sense that colour anymore.

#DrawingPlatforms

Flipping code

'I would like my class to create digital flipbook animations.'

Traditionally, animation was achieved by presenting the eye with slightly different still images quickly enough to merge into a moving image. While the frame rate is much higher in today's animated Hollywood blockbusters created using computers, the principle is still the same.

#FlippingCode

Demonstrate a paper flipbook animation to your pupils and ask them to create one as well. Tell your class that they will make a digital flipbook using Scratch.

There are a number of different ways in which they can achieve this. They could draw on paper and then take photos or scan their drawings into the computer. They could draw the drawings within the sprite editor, copy the previous image and tweak it so it's slightly different in each frame. They could also capture photos of themselves and move objects between shots, like in the 'Stop motion' video available in the Online Resources.

Once the images are ready, add them as one sprite with many costumes. Use a trigger, such as the green flag, to begin running through the costume sequence using the *next costume* block from *Looks* and the *wait___secs* block from the *Control* section with a short wait time. Because these are individual sprites, it's possible to have multiple sprites being animated at the same time.

Clone code

'We want to create building games where the player can create as many blocks as they need.'

Copy and paste is one of the most used functions in the computer user's toolbox. It saves time and prevents more typing mistakes than it creates. It is also useful in games so the player can generate seemingly infinite numbers of objects to use.

Your pupils should begin by thinking about games which require lots of use of the same sprite using the same code again and again. Good examples of this are games like *Bubble Shooter*, where coloured balls are shot from a cannon aiming to connect three or more of the colours together, or any shooter game where the same projectiles are used time and again. Building games are another good application, e.g. where one block in a menu can be clicked and the player receives that block to build with.

To clone sprites in Scratch, ask your pupils to explore the *Control* section. There are three blocks here which are useful for working with clones. Firstly, *when I start as a clone* is a trigger which allows the coder to differentiate the cloned block from the original, for example, making it draggable rather than fixed to one position in the building game scenario. The *create clone of____* allows you to create clones, not just from the block itself, but also from other sprites and triggers. There is also the *delete this clone* block.

An interesting practice activity is to create an ant colony on a green leaf backdrop. Code one ant to march around the screen with *pick random____ to____* code from the *Operators* section and *if on edge, bounce* from *Motion*. Use the *pen down* block from the *Pen* section to change the green leaf backdrop to black. Clicking the ant clones it. The green leaf background will soon be munched away by the ant army.

Teaching tip

Because clones retain the code of the original sprite, they can be very useful. Watch out for instances where having multiple sprites do the same thing could cause a bug. If this is a problem, pupils could change the code on the individual clones.

#CloneCode

Board games

'I want to create some classic board games with my class.'

There are many treasured classic board games which are superb to play in a digital form. Many follow logical rules and are therefore relatively easy to design.

Firstly, ask your pupils to think about the board games they have played. Discuss which games they think would be easy to code and why. Below are some of the key coding elements of two classic games:

Four-in-a-row, where players take turns to drop coloured counters into a grid to make a row, is a classic wet break-time game. Use the colour-sensing capabilities of Scratch from the *Sensing* section to animate the dropping of the counters into position using precise coordinates from the *Motion* section. Give each column a variable counter so the code *knows* how many coloured counters there are in the column already. At the top of each column, draw a coloured line which the counter touches and then follows a set algorithm to glide into position based on the column colour and the column variable. So, if it touches red, and the variable number for the red column is 3, it glides to the coordinates of space 3 in the red column. You will need to add a continuous downward movement using the *forever* and *wait___secs* blocks from the *Control* section and directional blocks from the *Motion* section.

Snakes and ladders can be coded in a similar way, with each player's counter being given a variable. Create a random number die using the random block from *Operators* to change the variable in turns. The variable signals to the counter a different set of coordinates to glide to. If square 4 has a ladder, use the *If* block to add, let's say 20, to move to the top of the ladder at square 24.

#CodingBoard

Crazy golf

'How can my class use colour sensing to create puzzle games.'

Golf and pool games were popular during the early days of game design as they can be created in 2D and rely on simple straight lines and turns.

Inform your class that they are going to create a crazy golf game. Discuss the features of the game they have played in real life. Discuss how they can simulate some of these within Scratch with code.

Ask your pupils to attempt to make a ball (sprite) transport from one end of a tunnel and emerge from the other. They could use *touching color__?* from the *Sensing* section to detect the colour of the tunnel entrance and move to new coordinates and then continue on the same path. Your pupils can set winning conditions by using the same method to trigger a winning screen when the ball is touching the hole sprite.

The children could add a strength variable from the *Variables* section which controls the speed of the ball. The ball can start at that speed and then decelerate by using the *change__by__* from the *Variables* section and the *wait__secs* from the *Control* section to bring the ball to a halt.

The coders can use the *point towards mouse-pointer* block from the *Motion* section to allow the players to aim the ball using the mouse.

Lastly, your pupils can take crazy golf to new heights with gameplay which wouldn't be possible in the real world. For example, add a slow *glide__secs to x:0 y:0* from the *Motion* section together with a *forever* block from the *Control* section to simulate a conveyor belt to the centre of the screen when the golfing hole is at the edge of the screen, making the game even more challenging.

Teaching tip

Allow your pupils to explore and experiment with coding and gameplay ideas to expand their games and their knowledge.

Taking it further

Add an extra dimension to your 2D games by designing your levels to be actual levels. Design a game where the goal is to drop an object down a hole, like a game of golf played on many storeys, with the next 'level' of the game being the floor below. Try adding a stairwell to adventure games or the depth of the ocean in a submarine game.

#CrazyGolf

55

Coding and literacy

Part 5

Coding stories

'I want to combine my class's love of stories with their love of coding.'

Many of your pupils will have played games based on books or movies. Crossing over media boundaries is not always easy, and either the gameplay or the storyline usually suffers as a result.

Ask your pupils to research games which have interesting storylines. Share these as a class and try to find examples online to share. Discuss what aspects of the story are good and talk about how the story and game play are interlinked, not 'bolted on'. Make a written list of these for the class to refer back to.

In pairs, ask your pupils to attempt to weave a story and a game together. For this activity the type of game doesn't matter too much, but the game should form a part of the story and advance the narrative. Ensure your pupils write a narrative and storyboard it carefully, knowing where game elements will appear.

Use either Scratch or the 3D game creator Kodu *kodugamelab.com* to create a game and a story. Particularly important will be narration captions and dialogue. Use the *say* function in Kodu or the *say* or *think* blocks from the *Looks* section in Scratch so the characters can express themselves and interact. The projects must have clues or instructions which instruct the player how to move on through the story.

Bonus idea ★

Create an educational non-fiction game which has a narrative. Follow the adventures of a famous person from history, a character in a real geographical location to explain what life is like there, or the story of a particular scientific discovery or event.

#CodingStories

3D stories

'I want to animate cartoon stories in 3D using coding skills.'

With virtual reality in its renaissance, 3D virtual environments and animations are becoming ever more popular and will probably be important creative endeavours in the future, as the big tech companies are currently putting a lot of funds into this area.

Tell your pupils they are going to do some puppeteering with a difference. Rather than doing this with puppets in the real world, they are going to use their coding skills to do this in a 3D virtual environment to tell a story and act out a scene.

Using Looking Glass at *lookingglass.wustl.edu*, ask your pupils to log in and choose a template from *New Worlds*. From the small-stage window, click on a character to begin to code. Just like in Scratch, Looking Glass uses blocks which can be dragged into the *My Story* area. The block can be found in three different coloured areas: *Actions*; *Action Ordering Boxes*; and *Questions*. Experiment with the *[name] say [text]* block from the *Actions* section and make your character say something. Try using the *[name] move towards [target] [amount]* block to move this sprite towards another. Press *play* on the menu bar to see the result. Movements can get very detailed, down to a sprite moving a hand or a limb to gesture and interact as they talk.

From the stage, click *Edit Scene* to change the starting positions of the sprites. Be sure to use the camera movement arrows at the bottom of this screen to manoeuvre the camera into a good position from which to organise the scene.

Once this is complete, click *Edit Actions* to return to the action blocks page.

Teaching tip

This explanation barely scratches the surface of what Looking Glass can produce. Explore the platform and produce a short scene of puppeteering with the virtual actors. Some amazing animations will result with a little practice and patience.

Taking it further

Put more of the responsibility for practising weekly spellings on your pupils by asking them, possibly a group or two at a time according to a rota, to create a game which helps everyone practise their spellings for that week. The other pupils can practise at home or at school using a web link to the Scratch project.

#3DStories

Epic gaming

'How can we create adventure games based on adventure stories in a 3D environment?'

The majority of console games are based in a 3D environment. It is now really only mobile gaming where most 2D games can be found. Rendering the graphics in a 3D environment requires a lot of computer power and shows just how much progress computing has made in recent decades.

Teaching tip

3D environments can be used across the curriculum in different ways. Use the landscape editing in Kodu to create geographic features, recreate stories from history or explore mathematical ideas with shapes and paths using the patrol commands.

Taking it further

Ask your class about their favourite adventure stories where the heroes travel vast distances and complete brave tasks. As well as producing some excellent code, you can use this work to develop extended writing pieces.

#EpicGame

Using Kodu at *kodugamelab.com*, ask your pupils to design a 3D world based on their favourite adventure stories. Kodu opens with the Kodu character in the middle of a small area of land.

Firstly, your pupils will need to expand the area of land available. Use the *Ground Brush*, which can be seen at the bottom of the editing screen, to create more flat land. Use the icons to the right to create undulating land to suit the epic adventure. Use the left mouse button to drag the screen to your desired position and click right and drag to rotate around the middle point of the view to change the angle.

Add some more characters using the *Object Tool*, which is near the ground icon. There is a lot to discover under this icon. For now, click it and then click on the land where you want to place the character. A circular selector will appear. Select the *Rover*, which should appear on the space on the land where you clicked. Next, right-click on the *Rover*, then *Program*, which should allow you to choose behaviours. Click on the + next to the *when* and the *do*. Once you have chosen the behaviours, press *Esc* on your keyboard. You can create goals, obstacles and enemies in just the same way. Click on the green play triangle to test the game and the controls and behaviour you have added. Continue to build, test, debug, repeat until the game is complete.

Spelling games

'How can my class use their coding skills to improve their spelling?'

Spellings aren't the most interesting thing to learn or to teach. Using technology and games may improve engagement, and it helps pupils to take a break from learning by rote.

Using Scratch, ask your pupils to design a spelling game. They could use the letter keys on the keyboard, but in my 'Spell code' example in the Online Resources, I have opted to have each of the letters on the screen so they can be clicked to select a choice. The letter then disappears and acts as a reference for the player for the letters that have already been attempted. This uses the *when this sprite clicked* trigger block from *Events* and the *hide* block from *Looks*. Note that this is just one level and that the word the player is attempting to find is fixed.

I have used a variable to state how many mistakes have been made. In addition, I have green button sprites which change colour to red when the variable reaches a certain number (in this case, six). Once six mistakes have been made, I have used the *broadcast____* to signal to all the letters to disappear to end the game.

Pupils might also wish to record audio of words and use blocks from the *Sound* section to play the audio, then use the *ask____and wait* and *answer* blocks from the *Sensing* section, plus a variables list for the answers. This will allow the game to mark whether the answer is correct or not.

Taking it further

Put more of the responsibility for practising weekly spellings on your pupils by asking them, possibly a group or two at a time according to a rota, to create a game which helps everyone practise their spellings for that week. The other pupils can practise at home or at school using a web link to the Scratch project.

#SpellingGames

Branching story

'My pupils want to expand and experiment with their creative narrative writing with coding.'

Creative writing activities are some of the great joys of teaching at primary school. Explore different formats and different ways to structure stories using digital technology by creating branching stories and a digital book.

Creating a multidirectional story is nothing new, and many pupils will have experienced books which ask the reader to turn to a particular page to make a choice about how the plot develops.

You can achieve a digital version of this using a hyperlinked website, linking between different slides on PowerPoint or Google Slides. For this example, I will use Scratch.

After planning their stories using traditional means, ask your pupils to choose all the sprites, objects and backdrops they will need for the story project. Use the *Green Flag* as a reset for the story. Your pupils will need this repeatedly while they are designing their project. Use blocks like *go to x:__ y:__* and changing the backdrop to ensure everything begins at the right position.

Coordinate the actions between many sprites by using *broadcast___* from the *Events* section. This means that an action, such as clicking on a sprite, can signal to other sprites to begin a range of actions. Use the *when I receive___* trigger from the *Events* section to allow sprites to react to broadcasts. Use this to sync a change of scene, sequence dialogue and much more. When the reader makes a choice for the branching plot, they can click on one item or another to trigger a broadcast.

See the 'Adventurous cat' example in the Online Resources.

#BranchingCode

Grammar games

'What can I do with code to create something to improve my pupils' grammar?'

Learning and practising grammar for tests occupies a lot of time at Key Stage 2 (pupils aged between 7 and 11) for both pupils and teachers. Much of this is learning by rote and completing page after page of paper-based grammar activities. Yet digital games and resources are becoming more commonplace in schools. Why not make your own?

Cloze missing word tests are a staple of grammar exercises and are easy to create in Scratch using *when this sprite clicked* from the *Events* section to hide a sprite which is covering the unknown word of a sentence. Ask your pupils to make a different exercise each for the other pupils to use for practice, and you will quickly have a large bank of digital grammar resources to use.

Multiple-choice questions are quick to make and can even be self-marking. Input the sentences or words which the user will need to choose between and ask your pupils to use some A, B, C and D sprites from the library. Use *broadcast* and *when I receive____* from the *Events* section to signal to other sprites whether the correct answer has been clicked or not and react accordingly.

A final common grammar activity is connecting two sentences, words, statements or answers together with a line. You could do this by using the *pen down* block from the *Pen* extension section and use a button and a *broadcast* to signal which choice has been made. This then commands the drawing sprite to move a given distance and direction to draw a line between two given answers.

Teaching tip

It may sound obvious, but your pupils are in the process of learning and practising grammar themselves and they may make mistakes, especially when their minds are focused on building the project. Ensure that the grammar activity is outlined on paper first and checked by an adult.

#GrammarGames

eBooks

'How can my class create eBooks to archive their stories forever and share them with the world?'

A well-stocked school library is a sight to behold, but an increasingly rare one. Bolster your book stock with stories created by your pupils, and create an archive of eBooks for your classes to read past pupils' work for decades to come.

While there are many ways to create eBooks, such as websites like *www.mystorybook.com*, Apple Books or using a blog, we are concerned with coding, so let's use Scratch as our medium.

Firstly, your pupils will need stories they have written and any illustrations they wish to include. They may also wish to include some animations in their eBooks. It's safer to write the story on a word processor first and copy and paste the text into Scratch in case it's lost during the coding process.

Add a title page, possibly breaking with tradition and adding a blurb to the title page to help entice readers to keep going. Add the text and media as backdrops, ensuring that the text size is appropriate for reading in full-screen mode. There should also be enough empty space on each backdrop in the same location on the screen to include buttons to control the eBook. If the book is short, your pupils can add a link to every page using number sprites and the *switch to backdrop___* block from *Looks* and a clickable trigger for each one. If the book is longer, they may wish to allow readers to jump in multiples of two or five, in addition to coding previous-page and next-page buttons.

Your pupils can add in any animations which they feel will add to the story, but make sure these are not distracting.

#eBooksCode

Forensic investigation

'My class are looking at the report writing genre and want to describe the things they discover from a crime investigation.'

WebQuest was once a popular educational tool, where users were guided through a series of website screens with images and text to learn about a topic. Make an interactive WebQuest, where details and information are slowly revealed.

Firstly, the class need to think about which mild misdemeanour they will design a project about. The idea is that the WebQuest slowly reveals the clues to solve a mystery.

Using Scratch, upload all of the images that you wish to use. Word process any text that you wish to add and copy and paste onto backdrops. Add 'next' and 'back' buttons to allow the user to control the pages. There may be some activities which are required before the user is allowed to progress. Your pupils may wish to hide the 'next' and 'back' buttons on these occasions. One such activity could be finding clues within an image. Make the image clickable and use a variable which will allow you to ensure that the user finds all of the objects they need to. The variable will need to be a certain number before the user is allowed to proceed. This can be archived from the **Variables** section. Your pupils may want to ask questions along the way too. Use the **ask___ and wait** and **answer** blocks together with the **equals (=)** sign block from the **Operators** section to require specific answers to questions before the user can continue.

There are so many different ways that this project could be done. Your pupils may wish to include animation, video control and drawing tasks, and even design games within the WebQuest.

Teaching tip

In my own class in the past I have used funny things such as: Who took our chocolate? The Easter Bunny was blamed. Who left sticky fingerprints in our classroom and took our teddy mascot? It was the Early Years class, naturally.

Taking it further

Have the users learnt anything for the WebQuest? Prove it! Ask your pupils to add a quiz or test based on the information within the WebQuest to assess what has been learnt.

#ForensicQuest

Fake news

'I would like to design a platform to share my pupils' creative non-fiction writing and news reports.'

Websites are a great way to share information with a wide audience. But, as highlighted in Idea 24, websites require a lot of knowledge to edit HTML. Thankfully, Scratch will do just as well.

Firstly, look at my fairy-tale news site at *ictmagic.wix.com/fairytalenews*. Your pupils should hopefully realise that these news stories are made up. Ask your pupils to write similar fictional news stories, using something other than fairy tales if you wish.

Once written, the children will need to source any other content that they wish to include. Using Scratch and working in pairs they next need to create a banner for their fictional news site. They will need to include the headline, a tagline and an image on the front page as sprites. Using the *when this sprite clicked* block from the *Events* section, make each of the news items clickable, and so they change to another backdrop and/or show and hide sprites as needed using the *show* and *hide* blocks from the *Looks* section.

Your pupils may also like to create 'video' using sprite animations and recorded audio. To record audio, they will have to go to the grey *Sounds* tab above the colour block sections. To play the sounds, they can use the *play sound___* block from the *Sound* section.

Bonus idea ★

Fictitious online biographies, persuasive writing and instructional websites are all possible in a similar way and give your pupils' writing a real audience.

#FakeCoding

Phonics sounds

'How can we create phonics resources for the younger classes in our school?'

Creating real resources for other classes in your school is a great way to provide an audience for your coders and work across age groups.

Firstly, if your pupils are in the upper years of primary school, a trip back to Early Years or Year One might be beneficial to remind them what it is like to start out on their literacy learning journey. Ask your class to observe a phonics lesson and to talk with the younger children afterwards about designing a digital resource to aid their phonics learning. The resource might take many forms, from flashing up words containing particular phonics sounds to a clickable phonics reference guide. Whichever direction your pupils' creativity takes, sounds and text are going to be needed.

To record audio in Scratch, they will have to go to the grey *Sounds* tab above the colour block sections. To play the sounds, they can use the *play sound___* block from the *Sound* section. Text can be added to backdrops, and they can be switched using the *switch backdrop to___* block from the *Looks* section. They can also add questions with typed answers using the *ask___and wait* and *answer* blocks from the *Sensing* section.

Active learning is usually beneficial for young children, and your pupils can create a game which requires the young learne\r to reach their hands towards a button on the video feed. From the *Video motion* extension section, use the *video motion on___* block to allow you to create buttons layered over video from your computer's camera and make the buttons interactive to a wave of a hand.

Teaching tip

Create competitive games with a scoring system using variables from the *Variables* section. These games can be two-player games with two sets of keyboard controls, or play one at a time and try to beat each other's score.

Taking it further

Once the games are ready, allow the younger learners to try them and give feedback. Your pupils should then debug and improve their projects based on this feedback.

#CodingPhonics

Dragging letters

'I would like my class to develop spelling games for younger pupils.'

We have explored hangman-style games for older children in Idea 49, but developing spelling games for younger pupils requires additional support and easier controls for them to use.

Brief your class on the requirements of the project, highlighting that the games need to only use the mouse and need to have no writing other than the word which the user is trying to spell. Suggest that audio might be an important element in the design of this game. Allow pupils to explore, experiment and develop their games in Scratch as they see fit. Here are a few ideas they may wish to try:

- Make draggable letters which lock in place when the letter is in the correct position or shoots back to its starting position if the letter is wrong.
- Use colour conditions from the *Sensing* section to code the letter to go to the correct coordinates of the correct block if the block touches the colour of the correct position.
- Your pupils can use very subtly different colours so users cannot see a difference, which therefore does not give them a clue to the correct answer. This can be achieved using the E-shaped *if else* block from the *Control* section. For the *else* gap, your pupils can add a *glide 1 sec to x:__ y:__* block to move the letter back to its starting position if the letter is positioned by the player incorrectly.

Record the audio of the word which the player will attempt to spell, including a simple age-appropriate sentence to put the word into context. Play these using the blocks from the *Sound* section and trigger them by the completion of the previous word.

Bonus idea ★

It's not just words which can be dragged into place, locked if correct or returned if incorrect. Number sentences or number bond pairs are also a great way to use this idea. Your pupils can even design a virtual jigsaw puzzle using similar ideas.

#DragCode

Coding and STEM

Part 6

Coding the body

'How can I encourage my pupils to use their coding skills to learn about the body?'

Computer programs simulate many biological systems to help researchers gain a deeper understanding of how they work. While your pupils' creations are not going to be greatly sophisticated, pupils will gain additional insight into how the body works and how it is put together.

Using Scratch, ask your pupils to design a version of the popular board game *Operation®*. They can begin by drawing cartoon versions of the body organs they wish to include (guidance advised!). For the backdrop, your pupils may wish to consider drawing the person's body on paper first and then taking a photo, or scanning the image and uploading it to Scratch rather than trying to draw this using a mouse. On top of the backdrop image, add some red lines and dots. These need to be spaced in such a way as to allow the organs to pass, but with only a little extra space allowance. Using the *if touching color___* block from the **Sensing** section, set the conditions so that if the body organ touches the red lines, the game ends. Ensure that the green flag resets the game back to the beginning and also sets the next game in motion.

To make the game a little easier for the player, instead of ending the game once the red line is touched, add a variable which deducts points when the organ touches the red line, but points are scored when it is removed successfully and is put in a holding area using the colour-sensing code once more.

> **Bonus idea** ★
>
> Design a learning resource where clicking or hovering over an organ brings up information about its function. Do this by using the **when this sprite clicked** from the **Events** section and showing previously hidden text sprites.

#BodyCode

Charting coding

'How can we use code to make a bar chart for our science experiments?'

Data charts lie at the centre of evidence-fuelled science, and the humble bar chart can express a wealth of information which words might struggle to convey at a glance.

Instruct your pupils to construct an interactive bar chart using Scratch. Set up a variable for each bar you wish to have. In my simple example (see Online Resources), I have just two bars, with a maximum height of four. Note that I have kept the variable number visible, but this can be hidden using the *Variables* section. I have used arrow sprites to control the variable, but your pupils may like to use the arrow keys of their keyboard or type the number directly. The bars change using the *hide* and *show* blocks from the *Looks* section and some 'more than'/'less than' operators with the variable. As the variable increases, more sprites are shown and a decrease makes them hide.

Shift from inputting data to recording it. Use your device's microphone to record the volume of the environment or the movement happening on your computer's camera.

Customise the bar charts with the objects which you are counting. So, for a bar chart about pets, you could use dog and cat graphics to show the number of pets in the class.

> **Bonus idea** ★
>
> Create interactive infographics which show information and data about a topic, but allow readers to explore how the overview changes if the data points change. For example, change the population size of Earth to see what area of land each human would have, change the units from metric to imperial by clicking a button, or see what increasing carbon dioxide levels do to the mean temperature of the Earth's surface.

#ChartCode

Cosmic coding

'How can I model a solar system in a coding project?'

Understanding orbits and how the Earth and the moon orbit around a common centre of mass is a difficult concept for young pupils, so visualising this is the best way to explain it.

Taking it further

Use a variable to change the values of the angles, wait times and motion size, and add buttons to the stage which allow users to change them easily without needing to change the code directly. Try adding a real element of gravitational pull by using the *go to___* from the *Motion* section and have the planets be attracted to each other as they orbit.

Set your class the challenge of designing a simple simulation of planets orbiting around a star in Scratch. Ensure your pupils know how to use the *pen down* block from the *Pen* extension section to draw an orbit line as the planetary sprite passes. They can also experiment using more blocks from the *Pen* section, which can change the colour of the lines. See my 'Cosmic coding' example in the Online Resources for this book.

Either upload planet sprites or find something suitable in the library. Your pupils should make sure that the planets are different colours so they can be easily differentiated. Use the *forever* block from the *Control* section together with forward motion, an angled turn and a tiny *wait* block value so it is a good speed to view.

Test and debug the values and starting positions of the planets. Use the green flag to reset the simulation. Set the starting coordinates and the directions of the planets using the appropriate blocks from the *Motion* section.

Lastly, select a starry backdrop for your simulation to improve how it looks. Consider adding clickable notes to the planets so that when a user clicks on the planet, it toggles *show/hide* text data and information about that planet.

#CosmicCode

Water code

'I want to create an interactive diagram to show scientific concepts.'

Use Scratch to build an animated interactive diagram of the water cycle, with pop-up explanations at each stage.

Before the pupils begin designing for interactive diagrams, it's important that they understand the processes of the water cycle, and therefore they should do their own research first.

Firstly, to make things easier, your pupils should create a backdrop which has every static part of the diagram on it to keep the complexity as low as possible. The sea, land and river do not need to be animated.

They should consider how they want to control the diagram with clickable features to show notes about different elements, but arrows or number sprites controlling the animations. Your pupils can use the *glide__sec to x:__ y:__* block from the *Motion* section to make the clouds move from the sea to over the land. Animated rain and precipitation could be shown as arrows that appear only when needed using the *show* block from the *Looks* section.

The clickable labels could use the same *show* block as above, together with the *when this sprite clicked* block and *broadcast* blocks from the *Events* section to make the information pop up and hide when needed.

Your pupils can record audio clips via the *Sounds* section, which can be found above the coloured block sections. Once recorded, they can add *play sound___* blocks to their code.

Finally, the diagram will need to be reset and the sprites will need to be put back to their starting positions, possibly using the green flag to trigger this.

Teaching tip

Because the stage is relatively small in editing mode, your pupils will need to make any text relatively quite large. The diagram will look crowded.

#WaterCoding

Coding craft

'I want to combine coding with spatial maths.'

Minecraft is a gaming sensation which most of your class will have played, most will play regularly and a few fanatically. It's a superbly creative game, but what can it offer for learning coding?

There are a few limited ways in which coding can be used in Minecraft, not only to push your pupils' knowledge of computing forward, but also for you to gain immense respect that you can teach them about a game that so many adore.

The commands will vary slightly, depending on whether you are using the full edition, Minecraft: Education Edition, Minecraft: Pi Edition for the Raspberry Pi, and so on. Once in the game, access to the command functions can be found by pressing the forward slash (/) key. Type */help* to see some of the most common commands.

Many of the commands have an element of maths embedded in them. You can change the time in your Minecraft realm. Type */time set 00000* for the sunrise, */time set 06000* for noon, */time set 12000* for sunset and */time set 18000* for midnight.

Another aspect of time comes from the weather command. Type */weather thunder 1000* to set the weather within the game to stormy for 1,000 seconds. You can also do this for *clear* and *rain*. After this, the game reverts back to random.

You can move your player great distances using xyz coordinates. Type */teleport playername 100 80 100*, replacing 'playername' with your actual username. Ensure that the y-figure (the middle of the three) is suitably large, otherwise you will find yourself underground and stuck in solid rock.

#CodingCraft

Coding weather

'I would like to create a weather map for my pupils to record a video forecast.'

Weather maps bring together many elements of design and coding. They are animated sequences which are triggered by the presenter.

Firstly, asks your pupils to watch a weather forecast and note the important elements on the class whiteboard. It is important to create a weather forecast sequence which is operated by a single person to model how this is done in real forecasts. The pupils need to think about how they can do this unobtrusively.

Using Scratch, upload or draw a map for the forecast region, and add this as a backdrop. There may need to be a number of these if the weather symbols are part of the image and therefore need to change. Your pupils may also wish to add the day and time to the backdrops.

Your weather forecasters have many different options for how to move the sequence on. They can use the computer keyboard spacebar using the *when space key pressed* from the *Events* section. Alternatively, they may like to control the sequence with gestures. See my 'Balloon Control' example of gesture control in the Online Resources for this book. This uses the *when motion>___* block from the *Video Motion* section as a trigger. This will allow your presenters to move the sequence on with a wave of the hand, plus they can see themselves on the screen, so they can point at items on the map while maintaining eye contact with your computer's camera if you are recording it. Place the button in the bottom corners to be less obtrusive for viewers.

Bonus idea ★

Scratch has many other uses around the newsroom. Create a teleprompter for news scripts or design backdrop sequences to appear behind the newsreader using the same methods and code used in this idea.

#WeatherCode

Experimental coders

'How can we use coding in our science experiments?'

Following instructions for an experiment is a great example of an algorithm, so take this to the next level and create the instructions as a coding project.

Ask your class to complete a number of science experiments, making notes on each step in detail and taking photos which may be useful in instructing others how to complete the experiment. Alternatively, you can find 13 downloadable science experiments to use via the Online Resources. Using these notes and photos, ask your pupils to create an interactive set of instructions for one of the experiments.

Open Scratch and upload any images your pupils wish to use. Create backdrops with the text. Create buttons for 'next' and 'back' to allow the user to navigate. Use *switch backdrop to___* from the *Looks* section together with the *when this sprite clicked* trigger from the *Events* section to move between the backdrops.

Using the same click trigger, make the photos clickable and add audio instructions and descriptions via the grey *Sounds* tab located above the colourful coding blocks area. Your pupils may also wish to animate aspects of the experimental procedure.

Lastly, your pupils can create an evaluation by using the *ask___and wait* block from the *Sensing* section with a trigger. Create a list called 'evaluation' for the answers via the *Variables* section. Also from *Variables*, add *insert___at last of evaluation* and place the *answer* block from the *Sensing* section into the gap, which by default says 'thing'. Repeat this for each question and answer. The answers for each should be added to the list to refer back to.

#ExperimentalCoders

Coding symmetry

'How can coding help to explore reflectional and rotational symmetry?'

Some pupils find it difficult to visualise different types of symmetry. Create an interactive quiz to make it easier for them.

Firstly, ensure your pupils have had some practice at coding the reflectional and rotational symmetry of 2D shapes. Using Scratch, ask your pupils to draw or upload any shape images they need.

Experiment with the default sprite to see how Scratch allows coders to manipulate the rotation of sprites in different ways. Click the sprite on the grey sprite window and you should see a blue and white information symbol, *i*. Click this and you will see that there are three different rotation styles. The circular icon means that the sprite will spin as it turns on the spot, so it will be upside down at 180 degrees. The left–right arrows mean that the sprite will flip. The spot icon means that there will be no visible rotation at all. You can set which to use via this screen, but you can also add the block *set rotation style___* from the *Motion* section. Use *point in direction___* and *point towards___* to change the direction the sprite is pointing in, with 0 degrees being straight up.

Create a series of questions which ask users to draw shapes when they are flipped in a mirror line, which can be checked by flipping and moving the shape to the correct position, ensuring that the drawing appears on top by using the *go backward___layers* from the *Looks* section. Similarly, create activities making shapes rotate on the spot and around a pivot point to develop understanding of rotational symmetry.

Swap projects with classmates to try them out and debug where necessary.

> **Bonus idea** ★
>
> Create a kaleidoscope project by using rotating shapes which are repeated in the four quadrants of the stage.

#CodingSymmetry

Animated matters

'How can I help my pupils visualise scientific concepts?'

Visualising the very small, the very big or the invisible can be difficult, even for adults. Create interactive animations with your class featuring these difficult concepts.

Firstly, ensure your pupils have a good understanding of the concept they are going to convey in their animations. Some extra self-directed research may be necessary to advance their understanding.

As a class, view some appropriate examples of science animations and simulations via **phet. colorado.edu**. Note that many animations are designed for learners much older than your primary learners, so choose wisely. There are more examples in the Online Resources for this book. For this example, I will outline how your young coders might create an animation showing the states of matter.

Use the ball sprite from the library in Scratch. Add just one to start, but once coded, you can duplicate and adapt the code. For the solid state, cause some jiggling by selecting a random direction using the **random** block from the **Operators** section, then moving a few steps in that direction before returning to a chosen set of coordinates.

For the liquid state, allow the balls to move everywhere in random directions as you will for the gas state. Use the **show** block from the **Looks** section to add a colour filling the lower half of the screen. Add the **if else** block from the **Control** section and the condition that if the ball sprite is touching white (the top of the page) using blocks from **Sensing**, it should point straight down and move in that direction. For the gas, remove the colour condition and increase the speed.

Multiplication square

'What can my pupils create to help them learn their times tables?'

Learning one's times tables is a rite of passage for all children. Help them to understand the patterns which underpin the tables by creating a tool in Scratch.

Firstly, take a moment for your pupils to practise their times tables in whatever fashion is the norm in your classroom. Consider how a standard multiplication square will help them understand the tables.

In Scratch, ask your pupils to create all 100 numbers needed for a standard multiplication square; these should be a uniform size, font and colour. Each one will be a separate sprite with two costumes. This will take some time. Insert numbers which look different in positions 1–10 down the side of the screen as clickable buttons; when the buttons are pressed they should trigger a *broadcast* block to signal that a particular times table has been pressed.

Choose any new sprite from the library that isn't a number to create the template code for the numbers in the square. Add the *when I receive___* block from the *Events* section with the table name in the gap. Add the *switch costume to___* block from the *Looks* section to change to the second costume. Do this code for each of the tables. You will also need a way to reset the costumes back to the first one.

From your template sprite, drag the code to the sprite in the grey sprite window which needs that code. For example, square 1 will only need the one times table, but square 12 will need code for the one, two, three, four and six times tables. This will be quite a logical task and may require careful testing and debugging afterwards.

> **Bonus idea** ★
>
> Create a random number-generated times table exercise using the random numbers from the *Operators* section. Use two sprites to say the numbers using the *say___* block from the *Looks* section.

#MultiSquare

Predatory code

'How can we create a tool to help the class understand food webs and ecology better?'

The complex interplay of predators and prey is not an easy concept for children. Removing any one organism from the environment can have catastrophic consequences for the whole ecosystem. Create a tool to simulate this.

Discuss the effect of invasive species with no predators, as well as habitat destruction, which often results in the large predators being lost first. Ask your pupils to explore the ecology simulation from the Online Resources. Your pupils should learn that the initial conditions are very important, and a slight tweak can cause the system to become a non-diverse monoculture.

Ask your pupils to create their own version of this simulator using Scratch and just one producer, one herbivore and one predator. Instead of a line graph, suggest to your pupils that they symbolise the number of each using the size of the image. Use the *calculation* blocks from the *Operators* section to decide the ratio at which the organisms increase or decrease when a trigger is added. The ratio will come from deciding how many creatures are needed to feed one eater. If you are below that number, the eaters will reduce in number (and therefore in size); if you are above it and they will increase. You will also need *if* statements to set the conditions. See my simple example, 'Eco Scratch', in the Online Resources. If your younger pupils are having difficulties with the maths, create a remix of the example and remove elements that they are unable to do. Use the resizing blocks. Write a range for them to try to give a sense of the numbers they should try. Test with a range of numbers and debug where necessary.

Coding and the humanities

Part 7

Code the world

'How can I create an interactive map?'

Maps do more than show us where to go. They give a locality a sense of identity and ownership over its information.

Taking it further

Add a search function to your map. Use the **ask___** and **wait** and **answer** blocks from the **Sensing** section to look for particular pre-assigned places.

Firstly, look at how maps are created online. As a class, discuss the important features you wish to have on your own maps.

If you are building these in Scratch, it is important to remember that, if shared, these maps will be publicly available to anyone, and therefore pupils need to be eSavvy about personal information.

To draw the basic map, your pupils may wish to use paper first and then take a photo or scan it to upload to Scratch. If they plan to make the map zoomable, the image will need to be fairly high resolution to avoid becoming pixelated. Alternatively, your pupils could draw a separate zoomed-in version of locations of interest and create clickable hotspots which allow users to zoom in at selected places only. Add the basic maps as backdrops to make switching between them easy via the **Looks** section. Use the **when this sprite clicked** block from **Events** to create the clickable areas and the **broadcast** blocks from **Events** to coordinate the hiding and showing of the clickable buttons. Make sure there is a way to zoom out and return to the main map.

To make this a guided tour, pupils will need to show an order to the places to visit using number sprites from the library instead of hotspots. To give additional information, your pupils can record audio tour clips via the **Sounds** tab, which can be found above the coloured block sections. Once recorded, they can add **play sound___** blocks in their code.

#CodingWorld

Building a quiz

'How can my class build a quiz which lets them know if their answers are correct?'

Assessment is one of the most important strands of learning, and independent learning requires it to ensure the learning is happening and to know what direction to go in next.

It is best to have a topic in mind for your quiz, rather than allowing your pupils to decide on a topic. This will allow you to choose something from classwork which everyone knows something about and to make sure it's educational. Make a list of five or six questions and their correct answers before you get started on the computer.

Using Scratch, click the backdrop square on the left-hand side of your page to select the script for the backdrop. Create a trigger to begin the quiz, such as the green flag from *Events*. Use the *forever* loop block from *Control*. This will allow you to keep asking the same question if the answer is wrong. Add an *ask___ and wait* block from *Sensing* and the accompanying *answer* block. Put the *question* block under the *trigger* block. From *Control*, select the *if else* E-shaped block, and in the diamond-shaped slot add a *___=___* block from *Operators* and place the answer block on one side of the equals sign, with the correct answer to your question typed in on the other. Note that upper or lower case makes no difference, but numbers like 4 and four will not both be recognised, so you may need to give some direction to users. In the bottom *else* part of the E-shape, place in it what you want to happen if the answer is incorrect, and in the top part place a copy of all of this coding, except for the trigger and *forever*, to begin adding the next question. See my very simple example in the Online Resources.

Teaching tip

Use lists from the *Variables* section to create multiple answers to a question to solve the '4/four' problem.

#CodeQuiz

83

Digital overlay

'How can I create a map-based adventure game?'

Combining digital technology with the real world around you has obvious benefits – see more ideas about this in the last section of this book. But for now, using maps of the real world in your computer game has obvious links to geography and history.

Create an adventure game based on your local area or school grounds. You could do this using Google Maps via *google.com/maps* – you can create a custom map with waypoints, but this doesn't require any actual coding. Instead, let's use Scratch.

Firstly, you will need a map, which you can draw and then take a photo of or scan into Scratch. Alternatively, use *openstreetmap.org*, which has a better policy on taking and using its maps for creative projects than other providers.

If you are using an area from outside of the school, identify good landmarks which can be used to digitally pin things too. If you are using your school grounds, you may wish to mark out the positions in the real world somehow, e.g. with cones. If you are using your local area, you can ask your pupils to use their imaginations to travel to different places and times.

On their computer screens, the children will see pins within the map which link to information and images about the topic they are investigating. These pins correspond to landmarks or cones in the real world, where they will find more information, images and, hopefully, artefacts and structures too. Both the real world and the digital add different elements to the experience. Once your pupils have seen your model of this digital overlaying experience, they can design their own.

#DigitalOverlay

Virtual school

'I would like to create an online virtual tour of my school and showcase work from my class.'

Virtual school tours are wonderful when they are available on the school's website. They are relatively easy to create and add real value for guests to the school or for the community who can see the school changing over the course of the year if the tour is regularly updated.

Show the indoor virtual map of Harry Potter's Diagon Alley at *bit.ly/magicstreetview* for an example of what can be achieved. The first step is to ask your pupils to take photos of the school in key areas, especially work displays, and make sure the position of each photo is in the direct line of sight of another one to help users navigate.

Upload the photos to Scratch as backdrops. Find arrow sprites from the library and add them to the stage, orientating them to point to the real-world position of other photos. Using the *hide* and *show* blocks from *Looks*, make each arrow pop up where needed, and make them clickable to change the backdrop to the destination photo.

Your pupils may wish to start the tour at a logical location, such as the front entrance of the school. Alternatively, you could add a map as the title page to the project and have hotspots for each of the locations where the photos can be found on that map. This could make accessing certain parts of the school easier, as the user would not need to click through lots of images to get to a place of interest. In this case, each photo would need some sort of back button to return to the map.

#VirtualSchool

Historical timelines

'How can we create digital timelines in a coding project?'

Timelines are a superb resource for historians or for anyone who likes a visual way to discover how events unfolded. Create a digital timeline to chart your events.

#CodingTimelines

Using a history topic, the plot of a book or the daily diary of your pupils, ask your pupils to list ten key events.

Ask your pupils to design a scrolling timeline. They should be allowed to problem-solve a solution for themselves, but there are two fairly easy methods they could try.

Method 1

Create one large image which extends beyond the sides of the stage and which will glide from one end to the other. Create clickable left and right buttons using the *when this sprite clicked* trigger block from the *Events* section. Each click can change a variable, which can be created and changed from the *Variables* section. For each variable number the x-axis coordinates shift by a given amount using the *multiplying* block from the *Operators* section and the *coordinates* blocks from the *Motion* section.

Method 2

This is similar to Idea 35 from earlier in this book. Use clickable buttons to trigger a change of backdrop where the timeline information would be written as though they were on different presentation slides.

Finally, your pupils could add images and then add audio narration to each event to play automatically when the page is moved or when a particular event is clicked.

Persuasive website

'My class want to build a webpage which highlights environmental issues and persuades the audience to help.'

Making someone do something can be tricky. If only the 'teacher's stare' translated into other mediums. In other situations we have to use our words, and sometimes images and photos, to persuade.

Ensure your class are clear on the urgent need to act on climate change, habitat loss and pollution issues. Ask them to watch child-suitable campaign videos from well-known organisations about these issues and browse their websites to see what aspects of their message are most effective. Then ask your pupils to work in pairs and narrow down a topic they would like to cover into something specific.

Once they have written the content and searched for images to use, each pair can begin using Scratch to build their page. They will need to include text and images on the landing page as sprites. Using the **when this sprite clicked** block from the **Events** section, make the different elements clickable so they change to another backdrop and/or show and hide sprites as needed using the **show** and **hide** blocks from the **Looks** section.

Your pupils may also like to create animations and record audio to support their message. To record audio, they will have to go to the grey **Sounds** tab above the colour block sections. To play the sounds, they can use the **play sound___** block from the **Sound** section. Ensure there is a clear call to action for the audience to take away.

> **Bonus idea** ★
>
> Persuasion begins close to home. You can use similar techniques to attempt to change behaviours in your class. For example, your class can create persuasive arguments for handing in homework on time, why a tidy classroom is important, and why an appropriate level of volume is conducive to a good working environment. I will leave it to you to decide whether to file their writing as fiction or non-fiction.

#PersuasiveSites

Town through history

'We are studying how towns developed through the ages and want to showcase our learning through a digital project.'

Creating elements of a project which pop up and disappear when a certain variable value is reached is a useful technique in game design, and it allows the coder to change sprites when a particular score is reached. But it can be used in historical simulations, too.

Firstly, ask your class to research the periods when particular features of a town developed in history – there were not many airports in the 1500s! Make a chart on paper showing when castles, proper roads, factories and round houses appeared and disappeared. Of course, some historical monuments are still with us today.

In Scratch, ask your pupils to create a variable called 'year' in the *Variables* section. Upload or draw buildings and infrastructure for the town for all of its history. If the buildings are directly replaced by other items in sequence, such as round houses being developed into Tudor housing then Victorian houses, this can be done using sprite costumes. Use the keyboard up and down arrow keys to increase or decrease the variable using more blocks from the *Variables* section. Using more blocks from this section, and the *hide* and *show* blocks from the *Show* section, make triggers for the buildings to show when a particular year is reached. This will require an *if* or *if else* block from the *Control* section. Ensure the 'year' variable is visual so the user knows which year they are viewing.

#HistoricCodes

Archaeological dig

'I want my class to experience an archaeological dig without bringing mud into my classroom. Can coding help?'

To conduct an archaeology dig requires expertise and the right tools to discover fascinating unknowns from the past. Coding can simulate the experience and begin to build the required expertise.

Using knowledge from a history topic the class has covered, discuss and choose artefacts which were key to that time period and its events. Find images of these and upload them or draw them in Scratch as individual sprites. Next, draw layers of sediment, such as grass, rock, mud or clay, as a block of colour. Add all these to the stage in the order in which you would like them to appear, or order them using the *go to front* or *go backward___ layers* blocks from the *Looks* section to order them.

Each type of sediment will require a different tool. Using an *if else* E-shaped block, ask your pupils to add a colour-touching condition from the *Sensing* section, with a *coordinates* block from the *Motion* section so that the sediment moves to that location once it has been clicked with a tool which reacted with the colour of the sediment.

At this point, a user could simply move any sediment layer with the mouse. Prevent this using a *forever* block from the *Control* section with a *coordinates* block using the position for when the layer is covering the dig area.

Lastly, make the historical objects clickable and so they trigger text or sounds about the object to appear to give the user the object's historical context.

> **Bonus idea** ★
>
> Cutaway diagrams, where the reader can see the exterior and interior of an object by lifting a flap, are common in history books and in many other subjects. Use this method to move a section of a historical building's exterior to one side to reveal the inner detail.

#DiggingCode

Coding currents

'How can we use coding in our rivers topic?'

The different stages of a river is a popular topic in primary schools, but unless you are lucky enough to have all three stages of a river located nearby, your pupils will not be able to experience these first hand. Create an interactive simulation of a river instead.

Firstly, ask your pupils to build a model in Minecraft. Failing this, try using banked earth and trenches in the school grounds, or use pieces of guttering. What do the children notice about the speed of the water and the steepness of the slopes at the three different stages?

Ask your pupils to design a river simulation. They will need to decide whether to place this across one screen and animate the journey (similar to the road for the game in Idea 33) or whether they would like to set each of the three stages on a different backdrop. The latter would be easier.

To create the river on three backdrops, your pupils will first need to draw each of the stages using the *paint new backdrop* tool on the left of the screen. The children should attempt to animate the water using the drawing tools from the *Pen* extension section to create continuous blue and white lines. Create one and then duplicate and adapt the code.

Create clickable hotspots which unhide information about features of the river, including text and photos. To create this, your pupils will need to use the *when this sprite clicked* block from *Events* and the *show* block from *Looks*.

Bonus idea ★

Create animations of geographic features, such as a retreat waterfall or the formation of an oxbow lake. Just draw each frame on a backdrop and then quickly switch from one to the next to animate.

#CodingCurrents

Our home

'I would like my pupils to learn about their local area and learn more about the wider world.'

When I was young I had a pen pal. We would send each other letters every few weeks and write about where we had been and what was happening in our lives. How times have changed!

Ask your pupils to begin to think about how they would introduce their local area to an overseas visitor. Tell them to conduct research about their local area and collate text, photos and images to use in a Scratch project.

They will need to create a title page backdrop to explain the project and then an animated page with 'next' and 'back' buttons using the *when this sprite clicked* block to navigate. In this project, they will create a page about their location, while not revealing their names to ensure eSafety. They need to include photos of the area and text explaining what everything is for an overseas audience. You, as the teacher, will need to add some form of contact information on this second backdrop page.

The project is then shared with the world. Ask other children and their teachers from all over the world to complete a page and add contact details on a remix version. Share via your blog and on Twitter. Tag me *@ICTmagic* on Twitter and I will also retweet it for you. Once their new version is made, they should share it with everyone on the listed page and using the *#OurHome* hashtag on Twitter. See how far it can get and what your children will learn about other places.

#OurHome

So last season

'We're learning about the everyday lives of everyday people through time, and we want to use code to showcase what we've learnt.'

Clothes provide a fascinating insight into the lives of people throughout history at every level of society, as fashion and utility change as constantly as new technology and techniques allow. Uniforms, finery and rags each tell a story.

Tell your pupils that they are going to create a dress-up game where players mix and match outfits. Ask your pupils to research and draw clothes for the time periods they wish to include. Ask them to draw a tasteful gender-neutral silhouette on top of which to place the clothes. For a very basic version, your pupils can add the silhouette to the middle of the page with the clothes sprites around the outside to drag into place.

Add functionality to this by snapping the clothes into place using the *touching color__?* block from the *Sensing* section to detect that the sprite has touched a particular colour and trigger it to go to some coordinates set using the *glide__secs to x:__ y:__* block from the *Motion* section. Click the same sprite again to make it return to its original position using the *when this sprite clicked* trigger from the *Events* section.

Take this a step further by using on-screen buttons instead of the colours themselves. Use the *switch costume to___* block to add a variety of colours for each item of clothing ... and don't forget to accessorise, people!

Bonus idea ★

This technique isn't limited to clothes. Try creating a historical building by dragging blocks and snapping them into place. In geography, create towns or the features of a volcano in this way, and practise spelling or maths by snapping letters and numbers into place.

#HistoryDressUp

Coding and the arts

Part 8

Ambient art

'How can my class code to create an abstract piece of music?'

Using sounds from the environment has been a common feature of art installations for many years, and the results can be stunning.

Taking it further

Once the audio is coded, your pupils can consider putting together a timed 'light show' of flashing lights which shine in time with the music. They can either use the **wait___** block and attempt to time the lights with the music manually or use the **when loudness>___** block to trigger when the code detects a loud sound.

Inform your class that they will create a piece of interactive art. Ask them to think about the sounds of the everyday – ambient sounds from the environment. Make a list of these suggestions on the class whiteboard. Either take tablets or laptops outside or source recording devices to gather interesting sounds from the environment and around the school. You could ask the class to locate and record sounds from home and ask parents to email these files to you.

Upload the audio files the pupils wish to use to Scratch. Ensure that the files have filenames which make identifying them easy, otherwise change the names in the **Sounds** tab. Your pupils will design a project which allows them to play each sound at the click of a button, and will also code a sequence of sounds to attempt to make something musical.

Select some sprites as buttons or use the **when___key press** block to use keyboard keys to play the individual sounds. Use these in conjunction with the **play sound___** block from the **Sound** section. Once again, use the **play sound___** block, but use the **wait___** block to add pauses where necessary and combine many sounds together one after another.

To create the sound sequence, use a trigger connected to a button or the green flag.

#AmbientArt

Coding karaoke

'Is it possible to create a tool which plays assembly music and moves a digital lyric sheet forward at the right time?'

One of the joys of working in a primary school is practising singing in the run-up to the festive season, when the school is filled with the sound of children singing and teachers getting increasingly 'shouty' as performance night approaches.

Coding can take a little stress away from rehearsals. Ask your class to design a project which plays the music and moves on the words at the right moment. Firstly, ensure the music is not subject to copyright restrictions. It's probably best not to share a project online just in case.

Use Scratch for this project. It is easiest if the lyric screens are created as backdrops and changed using the *next backdrop* block from the *Looks* section. For the basic version, use a trigger, such as the green flag, to begin the music and timings. Use the *wait___* block from *Control* to time when the backdrop needs to change in time with the music. Ensure that clicking the initial trigger, like the green flag, resets the project and allows the music and words to begin again in sync.

To make this tool truly useful, especially for singing rehearsal, the teachers using it will need to jump to specific points within the song. Code this by creating buttons which jump to a specific backdrop. Jumping to a specific time in the music is more challenging. Audio files must start at the beginning, have sound which you can edit and have different versions which begin at different moments within the song.

Taking it further

Go to the next level and make the music player controllable at a distance. Add gesture controls by using the *when video motion>___* block from the *Events* section as a trigger.

#CodingKaraoke

Sonic patterns

'How can I stop the racket of my class playing real musical instruments in my classroom and create digital music instead?'

As any primary schoolteacher will tell you, the mis-squeak of an overly enthusiastic recorder player is one of the most piercing noises known to humankind. But coding can come to the rescue.

Show an example of sheet music to the children and briefly explain how this encodes the music for the musician to read. Explain that they are going to do the same with computer code to tell a computer what to play.

Open Sonic Pi at *sonic-pi.net* and copy, paste and play the code available from the Online Resources for this book and instantly become a legend!

Take your class on a tour around the platform highlighting the main features – the code editor window being the most important of these. Spend a little time looking at the help area, as this will aid their independent learning later.

Showcase some examples and then let the pupils practise with the basic beeps and repeats. In Sonic Pi, there are many different ways to code the pitch of a note; the easiest is to set the pitch as a number.

Ask pupils to type in:

```
play 80
play 70
play 60
```

You should find that the computer runs all the notes at the same time. Chords like these are important, but just like in traditional music, pauses and rests are important too. This is coded by using the *sleep* operation.

Amend the code to include a sleep for one second after each note:

play 80
sleep 1
play 70
sleep 1
play 60

You should hear that the tones change, and this is what the numbers above mean. Experiment with different numbers to hear the different effects. Like the *repeat* or *forever* blocks in Scratch, there will be times when you want the code to loop and repeat. Ask your pupils to add the *times* operation as below. The '*4*' codes for how many times you want this section to repeat. You will also see that there is a *do*, as in 'do something', and an *end.* Think of these as being like opening and closing mathematical brackets, with everything between them happening, in this case, four times. Just like in maths, these 'brackets' can have other brackets inside them, creating some very complicated patterns.

4.times do
play 80
sleep 1
play 70
sleep 1
play 60
end

Ask your pupils to experiment with the parameters and listen to what happens. Try putting two more *play* comments next to each other to include chords.

4.times do
play 80
play 70
sleep 1
play 60
end

Finally, try to put together a number of *do/end* sequences to create a more complex piece. Your pupils can even try putting one *do/end* sequence within another to have loops within loops.

Teaching tip

Many pupils have difficulty starting from a blank canvas. You may wish to ask your pupils to encode a simple rhythm from the real world into digital music to get them started.

#SonicPatterns

Sonic symphony

'How can I use coding to create real music?'

In music production today, no song is left untouched by digital enhancement. Using code, your class can create real music.

In Sonic Pi at *sonic-pi.net*, the instrument is called a synth, short for synthesiser. If you type *use_synth* followed by a space, a list of all the synths should appear as a small scrolling window. Ask your pupils to choose one, and then type *play* and a number. It should look like this:

```
use_synth :piano
play 80
```

Everything that comes after the *use_synth* command will use the chosen instrument. Ask pupils to add more notes and some sleeps. Try adding some decimals to make shorter pauses:

```
use_synth :piano
play 80
sleep 0.5
play 85
sleep 0.5
4.times do
play 90
sleep 0.125
end
```

The code *4.times do* above allows you to repeat any code which follows four times and is similar to the *repeat___* block in Scratch.

Add in a different synth somewhere in the sequence, as shown here:

```
use_synth :piano
play 80
sleep 0.5
play 85
sleep 0.5
4.times do
```

```
    use_synth :fm
    play 90
    sleep 0.125
end
```

Your class can change the length of time a note is held in two ways. Use the *release* operation, which is similar to the length of time one's finger lingers on the piano key. You can also use the *sustain* code, which has the same function as the sustain pedal on a piano in that it controls the length of time it takes for the note to fade away. Ask your pupils to try both of them:

```
    use_synth :piano
    play 80, sustain: 2
    sleep 0.5
    play 85
    sleep 0.5
    play 85, release: 2
    sleep 0.5
```

Also try *amp* to change the volume, fading in with *attack*. To set fade-out time, try *decay*.

You can also use musical notes. Instead of the number, write *play* followed by a colon and the note. You can also include flats (*b*) and sharps (*s*). Let's add some to our code:

```
    use_synth :piano
    play :C, sustain: 2
    sleep 0.5
    play :Ds
    sleep 0.5
    play :Ds5, release: 2
    sleep 0.5
```

The last major component is samples. These are snippets of music and beats of various lengths. They are independent of the current choice of synth, so they are useful as backing tracks or beats. Ask your children to open a different, blank buffer page and to type *sample*, followed by a space. They should then see a dropdown list of all the available samples. Ask your class to try adding a variety of samples, synths, notes, sleeps and operations together to see what they come up with.

Taking it further

Pauses are not just used in music. Use the *wait___* block in Scratch to create pauses, countdowns, or timed audio dialogues.

Bonus idea ★

Once confidence is built using Sonic Pi, ask your class to showcase their understanding in a live session where they improvise and adapt a piece of music for an audience.

#SonicSymphony

Abstract art

'How can my pupils create abstract art using coding?'

Artists have always used new technologies in their art, and coding and digital devices are no exceptions. Create a masterpiece by experimenting with code to create interesting projects.

Taking it further

It is very easy to change the parameters and get a random design. Once they have had a chance to practise, ask your pupils to predict and work towards particular desired designs.

Show your class traditional paintings or drawings of still life art and quickly move to images of abstract art where meaning and forms are not so easy to identify. Ask your pupils to design a project which creates abstract art using code. This should be a completely open project where the pupils are allowed to explore their ideas and experiment. Below is one direction they may wish to follow.

This example in Scratch creates geometric patterns using random numbers and ever-changing colours. Start with a trigger such as the green flag. It doesn't really matter what sprite you use as this is really a drawing implement rather than part of the design. Firstly, add *erase all* from the *Pen* section to your trigger. This means that you will start with a clean page every time you start the code. Use a *forever* block from the *Control* section to repeat the drawing code. Use the *pen down* block to begin drawing on the virtual page.

In my 'Abstract code' example available in the Online Resources, I have used *change pen color by___* to shift the pen colour by 10 units, which creates a rainbow effect. Within a *turn* block from the *Motion* section, use a *random number* block from *Operators* to add a little randomness to the project. Lastly, add a *if on edge, bounce* block from *Motion* to ensure the sprite stays on the stage. You may also like to add a *wait* block in here if you wish to see the drawing process operate more slowly.

#AbstractArt

Music video

'How can my class create a music video to accompany their singing?'

Animation has a long history in music videos, and music has often featured in animated movies and cartoons. Use coding to create your own with your class.

Search online for animated music videos, where the song and the animation are directly entwined and interact. Nursery rhymes are often a good example of this, although your pupils may like to work with more mature and/or cool tunes. Tell your pupils that they are going to create a music video where the animation reflects what is being sung about. This means that there will be many transitions to new sprites, and they need to be timed correctly. This will require lots of time, effort and patience.

The first step will be to create the audio, and note which objects will need to be added and when. Your pupils may like to star in their videos, and they will need to take photos of themselves and anything else that is needed. Record or upload the audio via the *Sounds* tab above the colour block sections. Play the audio using a trigger, such as the green flag, together with the *play sound___* from the *Sound* section.

To animate the sprites to accompany the music, use the same trigger and use the *show* and *hide* blocks from the *Looks* section together with the *wait___secs* block from the *Control* section. This trigger should also reset the music video to the beginning and hide or unhide the sprites (send them back to their initial conditions).

Showcase the animations as part of a live show where the song is muted and the pupils sing and dance with the animation in the background.

Taking it further

Combine the animation with real video by exporting the animation and mixing it using video editing software. The music video could be part of opening or closing credits for a television show which your class produces.

#MusicVideos

Warhol colours

'I would like to create art masterpieces using coding.'

Art doesn't happen on the canvas or in the grand concert hall. It happens in the mind, and the medium is largely irrelevant as long as the piece of art has the ability to move us. Computers offer us another medium to be creative.

There are many ways to create art beyond simply using drawing tools. Ask your pupils to explore using code to create multimedia art.

The bold colours of pop art are a wonderful way to begin creating an interactive four-picture Warholesque project using code. Firstly, your pupils will need a photo. Talk about how they might compose their photo with a clear object in the centre and an uncluttered background. Provide them with a digital camera and ask them to take a photo of something they are interested in.

Upload the photos into Scratch and arrange them to fill the screen, leaving just a little space on one side for a later step. Using blocks from the *Looks* section, use the *set___effect to___* to create starting colour hues for your photo. To rotate through all the colours is 1,000 points, so you could set each of the four images to a different multiple of 250 to space them evenly. From the same section, use the *change___ effect to___* to rotate through the colour hues, using smaller values or the *wait__secs* block to slow it down if you wish.

Take it to the next level by creating controls to change to colours with buttons along the space of the one side we left earlier so the user can manually control which hue to view.

#WarholColours

Tuneful falls

'My class want to create a creative musical piece of art.'

Creativity doesn't fit neatly into boxes – it spreads across genres and takes what it requires from everywhere. Create an art and music fusion where objects move around and create sounds as they do so.

Look at my example in the Online Resources. In this project, the ball drops and hits platforms. Your pupils' fusion doesn't need to be precisely like this, but it needs to include interaction to create music or sounds.

My example uses a variable which can be created from the *Variables* section. The value begins at zero and increases after a set period using the *wait__secs* block from the *Control* section. When the ball touches a platform, the velocity reverses and the ball deflects to one side. This uses the *touching color__?* block from *Sensing*. Each platform makes the ball behave in slightly different ways. Once the ball reaches the ground, it waits for a moment and then reappears and drops once more. When the ball hits the platform, the *set__to__* block is used from the *Variables* section to momentarily make the downward motion variable change to a negative number, meaning that it goes upwards. See more on this effect in Idea 38.

Your pupils could create more entry points for the balls to appear and even make them clickable using the *when this sprite clicked* trigger block from *Events* and drop only when the user clicks on them.

Taking it further

Using similar techniques, create a pinball machine which creates sounds each time a ball hits a surface. Make the ball bounce off of the object in a new direction.

#TunefulFalls

Gaming art

'How can coding offer a new perspective on classic pieces of art?'

Art doesn't need to be static. Indeed, some pieces of art may have paint which doesn't move, but anyone who has seen Vincent van Gogh's *Starry Night* would never say that it's static. But we can change this to the literal sense of static too.

Ask your class to view classic pieces of art and ask them if it were a game, what kind of game would it be? Take the suggestions and guide them to suitable ideas and away from poor choices. (No, Georges Seurat's *A Sunday Afternoon on the Island of La Grande Jatte* is not a good choice for a beat 'em up game!) Ask your class to look at the game adaptation of Piet Mondrian's signature style available in the Online Resources. Someone has gamified the artwork into a game of ping pong.

Ask your pupils to explore how to do this for their own chosen masterpiece.

In Scratch, the ping pong example would use clickable triggers using the **when this sprite clicked** block from the **Events** section to operate the buttons which change the y-axis value of the panel. It would also use a colour-touching **sense** block to 'know' when the ball had hit the panel and when it had been missed and hit the back wall. There is also a scoring system which would use variables from the **Variables** section.

A few possible suggestions for gamified works of art:

- Vincent van Gogh's Starry Night Asteroids
- Jackson Pollock Paintball
- Kandinsky Composition 8 Pinball
- Mona Lisa Dress Up

#GamingArt

Virtual instruments

'How can we create virtual instruments using code?'

As anyone living in the same house as a new musician knows, virtual instruments have one main advantage — the earphone jack! While it's usually better to play the real thing, coding instruments offers an interesting challenge for designers.

Collect together some of the school's musical instruments and allow your pupils to explore their sounds and decide which they would like to replicate. See examples of virtual musical instruments in the Online Resources. They will need to record the sounds each instrument makes or simulate these in some way. Your pupils can record audio directly onto Scratch or upload audio files via the *Sounds* tab near the top of the screen above the coloured block sections. There are a limited number of instrument sounds and notes in the *Sound* section which your pupils could also use.

Once the sounds are available, draw or upload suitable images to be the visible instrument on the screen. If sections are required to make different sounds, your pupils can add an additional sprite and make it almost transparent using the *set___to effect to___* from the *Looks* section and select *ghost*. Use the *when this sprite clicked* block from the *Events* section and *play sound___* from the *Sound* section to make the sprite create the desired sound. The user will then be able to hit, tap or strike the instrument to make music.

Now that all the sounds are added, why not add a song bank and play a song using the individual notes in a coded sequence. In addition to the blocks above, your pupils will need to add pauses in some places. Do this using the *wait___secs* block from the *Control* section.

Taking it further

Once your virtual instruments are created, it's time for a recital. Code sequences of sounds and collaborate with other teams to make sure that the music is well timed and sounds harmonious together.

#VirtualInstruments

Visual music

'How can we create abstract visuals to be seen along with the music playing at the school disco?'

Creating visualisations to accompany the beat of the music is fairly straightforward and looks very effective.

Firstly, be copyright aware. In most cases, uploading music into different forms, like uploading to Scratch, is not allowed under copyright law, so make your visualisations reactionary to the sounds being picked up via your computer's microphone. This also means that it's a more versatile tool as it will work with any music.

Ask your pupils to think about what kind of visuals they would like to create. View my example in the Online Resources. The main components are a *set variable to loudness* piece of code that uses blocks from the *Variables* and *Sensing* sections. The *Pen* section blocks draw a constant line across the stage and the pen size and colour change based on the level of noise. For the disco, your pupils may also like to change the backdrop to black, as discos are usually dark.

This isn't the only pattern that your pupils can do, and they may wish to use the *set variable to loudness* block or change the size or the costume of a sprite using the *change size by__* or *switch costume to___*, which are both available from the *Looks* section.

The speed, direction and angle are other elements that your pupils may wish to change. Use the latter to create an interesting volume dial.

#VisualMusic

Coding everywhere

Part 9

eSports

'I would like to create sporting tournaments using the class's coding skills. Is this possible?'

eSports are increasingly popular, and watching others playing computer games has become a popular pastime. eSports do not need to involve a sporty game. Any game where players can play or compete head-to-head or by comparing points is enough. Increasingly, eSports are breaking out of the screen and being played using robots.

There are many different ways that your pupils can compete in eSports all of which advance their coding skills.

Bee-bots® are a common sight on the forgotten top shelf of many a teacher's cupboard. Breathe new life into these bots with robot racing. Create a grid of 10 cm squares or a town playmat with lots of clear landmarks on it. The game begins when a referee says a particular location in the grid or playmat. The competitors must then program their bee-bots, place them just outside the grid or map and allow the commands to happen. The winner is the bot which is over the position when the bot stops and the code is finished. It could take a number of attempts to reprogram the bot and set it off again. The referee decides whether the winning conditions have been met.

Try rover sumo wrestling. The aim is to push the opposition out of an area but stay in yourself. Pre-code a course which should intersect with the other rover and push it out.

Sphero™ is a popular spherical robot coding device which rolls along a coded route. Try using one to play competitive bowling with some light skittles. Add in extra curves and corners to the bowling alley to make it more challenging.

Bonus idea ★

Finally, become real eSports stars and upload videos of your pupils playing their games to *twitch.tv* or *youtube.com*, ensuring that digital safety issues are taken care of.

#eSportsCoding

Adding components

'How can I introduce my pupils to the Internet of Things?'

The Internet of Things (IoT) is coming. Soon, almost every device you buy will be connected to the Internet in some way, and the data that is generated will flow both ways.

Start with a class discussion exploring which devices your class have at home now and which they wish could be connected to the Internet in some way and why. Talk about connected pet feeders, home-monitoring cameras and connected fridges. Explore the pros, cons and possible dangers of an ever more 'smart' home.

Experience the Internet of Things first hand by using a suite of sensors which can connect to the Internet, such as those available through SAM Labs *uk.samlabs.com*. Use input devices, such as a light sensor, to capture data about the world around you and share this using a host of services, including connecting and coding Google Sheets via *ifttt.com* to record the data at set intervals. These input devices can be connected to other devices such as smartphones, which allow your light sensor to trigger a text message or an alert to inform the user when sunrise happens, for example. Data can also travel the other way, and you can connect to web services to make your components react. For example, in my class we set up the motor to move whenever someone was browsing the class blog. We then attached the motor to a mini-windmill which turned when the blog was being read.

Teaching tip

You can also add components to Scratch. Try adding a microphone and using external cameras or going to the *My Blocks* section or the *Extension* area and adding additional hardware.

Taking it further

Smart speakers, such as Amazon's Alexa, are becoming a regular feature of people's homes. Pupils can use their knowledge of the IoT to design simple voice activated skills, either through *ifttt.com* or via the skills section of the Alexa app.

#CodeComponents

Drone coding

'I would like to try using a flying drone with my class but I don't know where to start.'

Unmanned aerial vehicles (UAVs), more commonly referred to as drones, have exploded into the consumer market in recent years from their beginnings in military applications. They are a marvel to watch and a lot of fun to use. But, most importantly of all, they are an excellent vehicle for promoting the learning of coding.

Drones are developing at an extraordinary rate, and authorities are still grappling with the consequences. The law on this is evolving constantly in many countries, so before anything else, check to make sure you are on the right side of the law via *caa.co.uk/consumers/unmanned-aircraft-and-drones* and *dronesafe.uk* when planning any activities involving drones. At the time of writing, the law states that for drones weighing 7 kg or less, you should be in visual contact with the drone at all times, act responsibly, not endanger anyone or drop anything, and keep it low (below 120 m).

Ensure that your drone is suitable for the age group you are planning to use it with. Most drones can be controlled in two ways – manually and automated. It is the coding element of the automated controls which we are interested in. Check out the controlling app to ensure it has pre-coded automated flight capabilities.

Allow your pupils to experiment with the code for flying the drone. Keep the children at a safe distance while the drone is in operation, or they can even control the drone through a classroom window if this looks better on the risk assessment.

#DroneCode

Translator

'How can I use coding to capture and celebrate the diverse languages spoken in my classroom?'

Help pupils learning English as a second language by creating a digital translator.

Firstly, record sound clips in English and the non-English target language for the same set of words. Upload five or six of these to Scratch and create text sprites for both the English and target language words. Arrange all the target language words on the stage and make them clickable using the *when this sprite clicked* trigger from *Events*. The click will hide all other words and show the English equivalent using the *hide/show* blocks from *Looks,* plus the *broadcast___* and *when I receive___ block* from *Events* to signal and sync these actions.

In addition, add the audio to the project by making the language clips play each time a word is clicked, for both English and non-English words. This will require the *play sound___* blocks from the *Sound* section.

Lastly, make a game section within the *translator* tool using the *forever* loop block from *Control* to repeat questions if the user gives an incorrect answer. Add an *ask___ and wait* block from *Sensing* and the accompanying *answer* block. Put the *question* block under the *trigger* block. From *Control*, select the *if else* E-shaped block, in the diamond-shaped slot add a *___=___* block from *Operators* and place the answer on one side of the equals sign, with the correct answer to your translation question on the other. In the bottom *else* part of the E-shape, place what you want to happen if the answer is incorrect, and in the top part a copy of all this coding except for the *trigger* and *forever*, for the next question.

Teaching tip

Ensure there is a reset or back button to return to the main list of words! See the quiz example in the Online Resources for additional help.

Taking it further

Explore Scratch's Speech Recognition features from the *Extension* area to create voice translators.

#TranslatorCode

Digital radio

'How can we create a radio player to showcase radio shows the class have made?'

Creating a wider audience for your pupils' creative endeavours is always beneficial for putting learning into context.

Ask your pupils to put together a range of radio shows. Some of these will be talk shows, but there may be singing provided by the children, as well as news, documentaries and perhaps investigative journalism – so perhaps we finally find out what is really in the school's chicken pies! Include made-up advertisements, jingles, DJs and continuity announcements.

Your pupils should share access to all of the recordings so they can create an online radio app each, and the best one can be used to play the shows to parents and the community. Upload the audio files via the *Sounds* tab in Scratch, which is above the coloured-block sections, and try adding music from the *Music* section (found in the *Extension* area).

Your pupils may wish to add visualisations to react to the sounds. See more on this in Idea 89. The radio will need a number of buttons to enable the listener to choose which content to listen to. These can be clickable buttons connecting to the *play sound__* block from the *Sound* section. They can also add a text sprite to give a blurb about what the audio is about.

#RadioCoding

In-flight coding

'Our topic is flight, and we would like to code something to do with aeroplanes.'

There are many aircraft systems that you could simulate. They are some of the most complicated machines and require vast amounts of computing power to stay in the air, but we can make them simpler in Scratch.

Ask your pupils to think about all of the systems on a modern aeroplane. There are lots in the cockpit, and your class may wish to create a basic simulation of the flight experience by altering the angle of the sky's horizon using left and right turns to simulate the aircraft banking into a turn.

However, there is a much more familiar system which many of us have used – the in-flight information and entertainment system. Create a basic clickable title screen which allows the user to navigate the system. Next, add a map to the stage as a sprite and expand so it is much bigger than the stage and much of it is off the screen. Place an aeroplane in the centre and code the map to move about it using many of the blocks in the *Motion* section, including those for gliding to a set of coordinates.

Your pupils can also add animations and record or play sounds to simulate the in-flight entertainment. Record or upload sounds via the grey *Sounds* tab near the top of the screen.

Test and debug with classmates as necessary, and try a little role-play transatlantic journey to see how useful and user-friendly it is.

> **Bonus idea** ★
>
> You have heard of an in-flight information system, but what about an in-lesson information system? Ask some of your pupils to flip their learning and code a study aid for an upcoming lesson. Check through it before it goes live and the other pupils have access to it for the lesson to actually help them.

#InFlightCoding

Rewarding codes

'How can my pupils design a coding project for a behaviour chart?'

Having a visual cue to refer to is useful for teachers, and it's also a reminder for pupils to do their best to make good decisions. Let your pupils code their own reward charts and include whatever they think is important.

Taking it further

Micro-certificates and badges are currently in vogue in education. Ask your class to design micro-tasks and a system for tracking them for one topic for a younger class within the school (so your coders know the topic well already). The pupils must deconstruct the learning steps into small goals. Each time the learner achieves the goal, they gain points and/or a badge on the digital system. This should be tested with a real class and debugged where necessary.

Discuss with your class what aspects of behaviour are most important and which should be rewarded. The answers might surprise you. Talk about what makes a good reward chart and what it means to them to be recognised for a positive action.

Using Scratch, ask your pupils to design their perfect reward chart for four or six of their tablemates. Give them the freedom to develop their own input system, but it must work with touch if it is going to work on the interactive whiteboard. See my example in the Online Resources. This example uses a variable for each of two aspects for each child and is changed by means of clickable sprites.

Inform your class that you are going to use their systems to chart their behaviour for the rest of the day, starting from when the project is finished, so the pupils have an incentive to finish quickly and start earning. If the pupils get a certain score by the end of the day, they will earn a treat. But if the chart doesn't work and the score doesn't move – tough!

The next day, allow the class to debug any issues which were found while using their systems and then trial them for one more day with a different treat planned at the end of the day.

#RewardingCodes

Opening doors

'How can we create a project which showcases one piece of work from every pupil in the class?'

Create a set of doors which has a piece of work from a different child behind each door. An Advent calendar isn't just for Christmas, it's for work too!

A way to showcase one thing from each child on a single platform can be useful in many situations. Showcase one piece of poetry from each child in a birthday calendar. Have the dates of their birthdays on the doors, and make it a class ritual to open it on the big day for each pupil, or create an inspirational message to themselves for a possible future when they are finding something tough.

Upload or draw any images that are needed, and then use the *when this sprite clicked* block from the *Events* section to make each of the doors clickable. When a door is clicked, it can change the backdrop to one where that child's item is waiting. You will also need to create a back button to return to the main menu. The pupils may also wish to keep the previous clicked doors open by permanently changing the costumes of those sprites so they appear different to the non-clicked sprites.

The pupils may wish to include additional media on their page, such as audio of them reading from their work, or an animation which relates to what is on the page.

Bonus idea ★

Use the same techniques to code a game of *Guess Who*. You can hide the characters' faces using a second costume.

#OpeningDoors

Colour detector

'How can we design an accessibility project to highlight the additional needs of some of our pupils?'

Designing products for members of the community with particular needs can be both challenging and rewarding. Allow your pupils to experience this by creating an accessibility product.

Colour blindness in its many forms affects a sizeable percentage of the population. Ask your pupils to design a project in Scratch that will help users identify a colour, and ensure that the product itself is colour-blindness friendly.

Explain to the class what colour blindness is, and bust any myths the children may have about it. If you are able, invite medical professionals into the classroom to talk about how colour blindness is diagnosed and any other details which they can offer.

Begin to design the colour detector. Your pupils will need to use the computer's camera to provide an input of a colour surface. Do this via the *Sensing* section and the *Video Motion* extension section. Use the green flag trigger to begin the code. Add a *forever* block, and inside that an *if* block from the *Control* section. Add a *touching color__?* block to the *if* block from the *Sensing* section. Your detector will need some sort of signal to show when it has found a particular colour. In my example in the Online Resources, I have used a block from the *Looks* section to make the cat sprite say 'the colour', and you can edit this to say the colour's name. Note that this example is not very sensitive, as it is sensing only one precise colour number. You could create more duplicate code to detect other similar colours. You could also use a variable to swipe through a range of colour number values for more sensitivity.

#ColourDetector